D1556882

Work for all or mass unemployment?

This book is dedicated to Daisy and to Gwen, who will face the European Labour market in the twenty-first century.

Work for all or mass unemployment?

Computerised technical change into the twenty-first century

Chris Freeman and Luc Soete

PINTER
PUBLISHERS
LONDON, NEW YORK

Distributed in the USA and Canada by St. Martin's Press Inc

Pinter Publishers
25 Floral Street, Covent Garden, London, WC2E 9DS, United Kingdom

First published in Great Britain 1994

Distributed exclusively in the USA and Canada by St. Martin's Press, Inc., Room 400, 175 Fifth Avenue, New York, NY10010, USA

Chris Freeman and Luc Soete are hereby identified as the author of this work as provided under Section 77 of the Copyright, Designs and Patents Act 1988.

British Library Cataloguing in Publication Data

A CIP catalogue record for this book is available from the British Library

ISBN   1 85567 255 3 (hb)
       1 85567 256 1 (pb)

Library of Congress Cataloging-in-Publication Data

Freeman, Christopher.
    Work for all or mass unemployment? : computerised technical
change into the 21st century / Chris Freeman and Luc Soete.
       p.   cm.
    Includes bibliographical references and index.
    ISBN 1-85567-255-3 (hc.). -- ISBN 1-85567-256-1 (pbk.)
1. Labor supply--Effect of technological innovations on-Forecasting.
2.Technological unemployment--Forecasting. 3. Employment forecasting.
4. Twenty-first century --Forecasts.
I. Soete, Luc. II. Title.
HD6331. F67 1994
331. 13'7042--dc20   94-13742
                                                                  CIP

Typeset by Saxon Graphics Ltd, Derby
Printed and bound in Great Britain by Biddles Ltd of Guildford and King's Lynn

Contents

List of figures

List of tables

Acknowledgements

We are grateful to many colleagues in Maastricht Economic Research Institute on Innovation and Technology (MERIT) in the University of Limburg and in the Science Policy Research Unit (SPRU) in the University of Sussex for advice and assistance on various questions. We would also like to thank IBM Europe for their sponsorship of our earlier research project on this topic and Carol Reavis Pillet-Will for much helpful information and suggestions. We are also grateful for helpful advice from Kay Andrews (Education Extra) and Geoff Mulgan (DEMOS) on education and ICT (Chapter 7), to Joyce Wood and to various firms for assistance in our research on the future of software employment. We alone however are responsible for the views expressed. Finally, and most of all, we would like to thank Susan Lees, Mieke Donders and Mariolejn Caniëls for their amazingly patient and efficient handling of the preparation of the text, figures and tables, which make the publication possible.

Chris Freeman and Luc Soete

1

'DISTURBING PERHAPS ALARMING': why mass unemployment is not just economically wasteful but also socially disastrous

1.1 Outline of the book

This is a book about technology and unemployment. In particular, it is about computer and telecommunication technology and their employment effects. Following this first introductory chapter, we summarise in Chapter 2 the prolonged debate among economists about technical change and unemployment. This was already a topic of controversy in the seventeenth century but it came to a head with the famous comments by the great classical economist David Ricardo in 1821 in his chapter 'On machinery' from his *Principles of Political Economy and Taxation*, in which he appeared to justify the fears of mechanisation 'entertained by the labouring class'. Like Ricardo, we shall argue that although in the long run technical change generates new employment to compensate for the loss of old jobs, it does not always do so quickly or in a way which is agreeable for the unemployed and their families. After discussing the contribution of Keynes and the neo-classical economists to the debate, we conclude that a synthesis is needed between their ideas and Schumpeter's (1939) theory of successive industrial revolutions. The diffusion of radically new technologies through the economic system is accompanied by crises of structural adjustment, as society adapts to the rise of new industries, new skills, new forms of work organisation and new technology.

In Chapter 3 we examine the main characteristics of the present wave of technical change, described by George Gilder (1993) as the 'biggest technological Juggernaut that ever rolled'. We present some evidence on the technical and economic characteristics of new information and telecommunication technology, which do indeed justify his description, and we discuss the contemporary problems of employment and structural change associated with the diffusion of this extraordinarily pervasive and influential technology. Just because in previous waves of technical change job creation has ultimately outstripped job loss, it does not follow that this will inevitably be the case in the future. Human history is a unique process and there are a number of completely new features of the present stage of evolution of the world economy. Some of these new features are discussed in Chapters 4, 5 and 6.

Chapter 4 deals with the new developments in the international division of labour, international trade and international investment flows. In particular, it deals with the rapid growth of the economies of Eastern and Southern Asia and the shift in the balance of world economic power from the Atlantic to the Pacific rim countries. This structural change in the pattern of world manufacturing exports confronts Europe and North America with entirely new problems.

'Flexibility' is a portmanteau word which carries many different meanings to different people. Chapter 5 discusses the question of 'flexibility' in wages, in work organisation and in patterns of employment over the working lives of men and women. The new patterns of working hours which have been spreading in the industrialised countries are associated with the growth of female (largely part-time) employment and the relative decline of male (largely full-time) employment. Changes in family life, womens' attitudes, management practices and new technology have all contributed to these profound social changes. 'Full employment' is not what it used to be.

Chapter 6 deals with the threats to the global environment associated with a pattern of economic growth based on energy-intensive and materials-intensive technologies. It argues that information technology offers some serious possibilities of ameliorating these threats and easing the transition to a more sustainable path of economic development as well as higher levels of employment.

We conclude from the discussion in Chapters 3, 4, 5 and 6 that a return to high levels of employment depends upon the policies which are followed to cope with all these new developments. Economists have rightly identified 'compensation mechanisms' at work in market economies through which job losses in one firm or in one sector are ultimately compensated by the growth of employment elsewhere in the system, provided aggregate demand is sustained at a sufficiently high level. The policies advocated by Keynes (1936) and Beveridge (1944) were designed to sustain aggregate demand at this necessary level and there are now some welcome signs of a return to Keynesian analysis. For example, Samuel Brittan in his weekly articles in *The Financial Times* drew attention to the problems of weakness in world-wide aggregate demand in 1993 and argued that this danger out-weighed that of inflationary pressures:

for the time being the greater threat is one of global depression — by which I do not mean a repeat of the Great Depression of the 1930s, but a drawn-out under-performance of output and employment, politically as well as economically debilitating. ('The worldwide threat of weak demand', *Financial Times*, 4 November 1993)

Galbraith (1992) in his book *The Culture of Contentment* has pointed to the danger that this prolonged underperformance could be reinforced by a political coalition of those social groups who actually benefit con-siderably from a period of high interest rates, slow growth and high unemployment. However, other economists have been quick to point to the fears of renewed inflationary pressures once recovery began in the United States and elsewhere. Moreover, the experience of the last 20 years has shown that Keynesian remedies are insufficient in them-selves. Although Keynes was of course right in his famous remark that 'In the long run we are all dead', it certainly does not follow that all long-term problems can be ignored. Many of the problems dis-cussed in Chapters 3 to 6 are quintessentially long-term problems, especially those relating to the environment and to technical change. The policy problems which are discussed in Chapter 7 are therefore a mixture of short-term, medium-term and long-term policies. Keynesian prescriptions alone are not enough.

1.2 Disquieting features of unemployment in the early 1990s

In times of economic recession new technology is often blamed for unemployment. This was the case in the 1820s and 1830s, in the 1880s, in the 1930s and again in the 1980s. Because of its pervasive applica-tions in every bank, factory and office, Information and Communication Technology (ICT) is often singled out for criticism today. For example, the mass tabloid the *Daily Express* on 11 February 1994 carried a feature article by Julia Finch entitled 'The price we are paying for the rise of new technology' which reported that:

Up to 45,000 employees face the chop in the City. The roll-call of redun-dancies seems endless.

Yet it is not recession that is throwing thousands out of work and on to the dole queues. No, these workers are the victims of the hi-tech indus-trial revolution that has been sweeping Britain.

If a machine or computer can do a job more efficiently and cheaply than an employee, it is inevitable that it will be used. And there are now fears that the new supercomputers will steal the next generation's jobs as well.

Captains of industry have already been warning that we must come to terms with the rapid development of technology and change working patterns to cope with the switch from labour-intensive manual jobs to the service sectors.

During every recession there is a jobs shake-out as firms struggle to increase productivity. But this time the purge has been compounded by the rapid pace of technology, which is taking over hundreds of paper-shuffling, record-keeping and manual jobs every day.

(italics kept from original)

Much has already been written about this subject, both by ourselves and others (see the References). If, therefore, we turn once more to this topic it is for three main reasons: the continuing explosive rate of technological change, the scale of social and economic change, and the persistence of heavy unemployment, especially in Europe.

In 1985 the world economy was just emerging from a deep reces-sion and there were high hopes that the levels of unemployment experienced in the 1980s would not recur in this century at least. Yet in the 1990s this level of unemployment has been surpassed in depth and in duration in many countries (Table 1.1). Moreover, there are a number of features of the present pattern of unemployment which were described by the Secretary General of the OECD as 'disturbing, perhaps alarming' in his Report to Ministers in June 1993.

Among those features are the high levels of youth unemployment, the high proportion of long-term unemployed, especially in Europe, and the high incidence of unemployment amongst those with lower educational qualifications (Table 1.2). The aggregate levels of unem-ployment, as shown in Table 1.1 were comparable, at least in Europe, to those experienced in the Great Depression of the 1930s. The figures shown in that table are not precisely comparable between the 1930s and the post-war period but they do indicate the approximate levels. Moreover, the statistics for the 1990s understate the true levels of unemployment for several reasons. First of all, the phenomenon of 'discouraged workers' leads to many workers not being officially reg-istered and counted as unemployed. The Annual Review of the OECD (1993) entitled *Employment Outlook* stated:

Open unemployment as measured through the unemployment rate captures a major part but not all of the labour market slack that exists in OECD countries. Slack in the form of discouragement and involuntary part-time work is substantial, equivalent to almost half the number of unemployed in 1991, or roughly 13 million people. Both tend to be cyclical, indicating that in a downturn the unemployment rate further underestimates the amount of labour market slack. (p. 17)

Table 1.1 Unemployment in various countries, 1933–1994
(as % of the labour force)

Country	1933	1959–67 average	1982–92 average	1992	1993	Forecast 1994
Belgium	10.6	2.4	11.3	10.3	12.1	13.0
Denmark	14.5	1.4	9.1	11.1	12.1	11.9
France	4.5*	0.7	9.5	10.4	11.7	12.4
Germany	14.8	1.2†	7.4	7.7	8.9	10.1
Ireland	na	4.6	15.5	17.2	17.6	17.8
Italy	5.9	6.2	10.9	10.7	10.2	11.1
Netherlands	9.7	0.9	9.8	6.8	8.3	9.3
Spain	na	2.3	19.0	18.4	22.7	23.8
UK	13.9	1.8	9.7	10.1	10.3	10.0
Austria	16.3	1.7	3.5	3.7	4.2	5.3
Finland	6.2	1.7	4.8	13.1	18.2	19.9
Norway	9.7	2.1	3.2	5.9	6.0	5.9
Sweden	7.3	1.3	2.3	5.3	8.2	8.8
Switzerland	3.5	0.2	0.7	2.5	4.5	5.0
USA	24.7	5.3	7.1	7.4	6.9	6.5
Canada	19.3	4.9	9.6	11.3	11.2	11.0
Japan	na	1.5	2.5	2.2	2.5	2.9
Australia	17.4	2.2	7.8	10.7	10.9	10.4

* 1936   na = not available.
† The Federal Republic for the period 1959–92.
Source: Maddison (1991) and OECD (1993), *Employment Outlook.*

Secondly, a number of countries have made revisions to their methods of estimating unemployment, most of which have led to a reduction of 'official' unemployment by transferring some categories previously designated as 'unemployed' to such categories as invalidity and sickness, retirement or training. In the United Kingdom, for example, more than a dozen such revisions have been made since 1979, almost all of which have led to a reduction in the numbers officially included as unemployed.

Table 1.2 The profile of OECD (1992) unemployment

| | Unemployment rates | | | | Ratio of lower secondary education unemployment rate to total rate[2] | Long-term unemployed as a share of total unemployment[3] (per cent) |
	Total (standardised definition)	Total[1]	Youth	Women		
North America	7.7	7.8	14.6	7.3	—	6.4
Canada	11.2	11.3	17.8	10.4	1.5	7.2
United States	7.3	7.4	14.2	6.9	2.3	6.3
Japan	2.2	2.2	4.5	2.2	2.7	17.9
Oceania	10.6	10.7	19.5	9.9	—	24.3
Australia	10.7	10.8	19.7	10.0	1.6	24.9
New Zealand	10.3	10.2	18.5	9.5	—	21.3
European Union	9.4	9.5	18.4	11.5	—	45.8
Belgium	7.8	8.2	17.6	12.2	1.3	61.6
Denmark	—	9.5	11.4	10.8	1.7	31.2
France	10.2	10.0	21.8	12.5	1.3	38.7
Germany	4.8	4.5	4.0	5.1	2.0	45.5
Greece	—	9.2	—	15.4	—	47.0
Ireland	16.1	17.8	27.6	19.4	1.1	60.3
Italy	10.5	10.1	27.9	15.7	0.9	67.1
Luxembourg	—	1.9	3.8	2.8	—	28.3
Netherlands	6.7	6.7	10.6	8.7	1.0	43.0
Portugal	4.1	4.8	10.3	6.5	1.7	38.3
Spain	18.1	18.0	32.5	25.5	1.2	49.1
United Kingdom	10.0	10.8	17.0	9.2	1.8	28.1
EFTA	—	5.5	9.3	5.0	—	12.9
Austria[4]	—	3.6	3.6[5]	3.8	—	15.2
Finland	13.0	13.1	23.5	10.7	1.4	9.1
Norway	5.9	5.9	13.9	5.2	1.1	20.6
Sweden	4.8	4.8	10.8	3.8	1.4	4.4
Switzerland[6]	—	2.7	4.7	3.4	—	19.8
Turkey7	—	7.8	15.2	7.2	1.5	39.2

[1] Comparable unemployment rates for the EC countries and national estimates for the other countries.
[2] For adults aged 25–64. Data refer to 1989 for all countries, except Japan (1987), Denmark (1988), the Netherlands (1990) and Turkey (April 1990).
[3] Long-term unemployed refers to all persons unemployed in 1991 for 12 months or more.
[4] Unemployment rates refer to the first half of 1992.
[5] Estimated.
[6] All data refer to the second quarter of 1992.
[7] Unemployment rates refer to October 1992.

Source: OECD (1993).

Finally, in Japan, Italy and to an even greater extent in some Third World countries, during recessions both company and national policies lead to the retention of workers who are seriously under-employed. In the case of Japan, some economists have estimated that if Japanese employers followed American management practice, then under-employment in that country would vary between 2 and 10 per cent rather than between 2 and 3 per cent of the labour force, as in the official statistics. In Third World countries there are often huge numbers of under-employed people in agriculture, as well as many under-employed in shanty towns. In South Africa the Central Bank estimated unemployment in 1993 at over 40 per cent.

During the 1930s, the extremely high levels of unemployment, coupled with the absence in many countries of adequate social security systems, led to deep political and social turmoil. The number of unemployed workers in Germany rose from 3.8 per cent of the labour force in 1928 to 17 per cent in 1932 (Maddison, 1991). At the same time, the vote for the National Socialist German Workers' Party (Nazis), which never amounted to more than a few million in the 1920s, surged upwards in the 1930s, peaking at 13 million in 1932. This was still not a majority of the German electorate but it was sufficient to give the ageing President Hindenburg the pretext to appoint Hitler as Reichschancellor in January 1933. The paramilitary formations of the Nazi party, the SA and SS, recruited on a large scale from the ranks of the young unemployed between 1930 and 1933. Similar developments took place in many other European countries.

There is a disquieting similarity between those times and the contemporary rise of racist and nationalistic movements all over Europe today, often focusing on problems of immigration and unemployment. Other disquieting similarities may be found in rates of crime and in suicide rates. As Galbraith (1954) pointed out, the incidence of suicide was actually never very high amongst bankers after the Wall Street crash but it did rise in the families of unemployed workers.

Some of these disquieting features are summarised in Table 1.3, but this by no means exhausts the novel features of the present recession. Not only is unemployment more severe and affecting some countries such as Sweden and Finland, which were relatively immune in the 1980s, but it is affecting new sections of the work-force, notably middle management and other white-collar workers. In particular, large firms have been making determined efforts to slim down their work-force and have indeed done so on an unprecedented scale. Hardly a day went by in 1993 and 1994 without an announcement by one or other large firm of job reductions in Europe, the United States or even Japan.

Table 1.3 Extract from the OECD Report to Ministers on Unemployment

The seriousness of the present situation

There are thus a number of disturbing, perhaps alarming, aspects of the current situation:

— In EFTA and in the European community until relatively recently almost no job growth occurred in the private sector, virtually all taking place in the noncommercial public sector. So far, significant reversal of this trend has been seen only in (the western part of) Germany, the Netherlands and the United Kingdom.
— The present recession-induced increase in unemployment comes on top of already-high inherited structural unemployment. In the European Community, unemployment appears to be 'ratcheting up' from each cyclical trough to the next. As a result, almost half of the unemployed have been out of work for 12 months or more.
— The United States unemployment has been more cyclical. Longer-term structural problems have nevertheless manifested themselves, both in a secular fall of real wages below a (normatively set) poverty threshold for low-skilled workers, and in the withdrawal of significant numbers of prime-age male workers from the labour force.
— The EFTA countries, which hitherto had been successful in maintaining full employment, are now experiencing drops in employment and rises in unemployment, in some cases dramatically so.
— During the recent recession job losses for low-skilled workers have occurred not only in manufacturing but also in the service sectors.
— Youth unemployment remains stubbornly high in many countries, notwithstanding significant youth programmes and the receding effects of the baby boom.
— Last, this poor labour market situation is rendering the effective integration of legally admitted immigrants more difficult, adding to social tensions.

Source: OECD (1993), p. 20.

As *The Economist* observed in an editorial (17 July 1993):

even companies still earning healthy profits have eliminated thousands of jobs, and are wielding the axe most enthusiastically among the middle-ranking, white-collar staff on whom they rely most for their success. With extraordinary zeal, western firms have embraced the idea that the best way to cope with a fast-changing world is not only to slash jobs, but also to scrap any promise of long-term, full-time employment to surviving employees, and then to demand more effort and risk-taking from those same people. At the stroke of a pen, many have been turned into subcontractors or 'consultants'. Those still on the payroll are being 'empowered' to make their own decisions and told that their future depends on the success or failure of their teams, not on the company's overall health.

As a consequence of these changing strategies of management, affecting also the public sector, especially in Britain and North

America, the *fear* of unemployment is probably now more widespread than at any time since the 1930s. Surveys of the British work-force have shown that more than half the labour force entertain this fear (e.g. *Financial Times*, 2 August 1993) and many economists attribute the sluggishness of consumer expenditure in the early 1990s to its depressing effects.

Economists have always recognised the waste of resources associated with high unemployment but in the 1970s and 1980s there was a tendency to give a higher priority to other goals of economic policy, especially reduction of inflationary pressures and international trade competitiveness. Whereas in the 1950s and 1960s full employment was emphasised as one of the principal objectives of most governments, relatively high levels of unemployment were increasingly tolerated as a necessary evil or even as a supposedly necessary spur to greater efforts, or wage restraint.

Now these attitudes are more frequently challenged and the vital importance of reducing unemployment levels is very widely recognised. The member governments of the OECD, which include virtually all the richer industrialised countries, mandated the Secretary General and his staff to prepare a major report on this topic in 1993–4. Their Interim Report in June 1993 showed that the issue of unemployment is now rising once more to the top of the policy agenda and the so-called 'Jobs Summit' of the G7 in March 1994 signalled the same concern. As indicated already, the reasons for this are not simply economic. Indeed the main reasons for treating unemployment as a top-priority problem are social, political and psychological, as well as economic.

1.3 The social consequences of high and prolonged unemployment

As the example of Germany in the 1930s has already suggested, social, political and economic aspects of unemployment are indeed difficult to disentangle. When unemployment rises all kinds of social tensions increase because of the psychological effects on the unemployed workers and their families. Marie Jahoda was one of the first social psychologists to observe and measure these psychological effects in an industrial area of Austria which suffered from extremely high levels of unemployment already in the 1930s (Marienthal). Her book (Jahoda et. al. 1933) is a classic and was translated and reprinted in several European countries in the 1970s and 1980s.

Marie Jahoda (1982, 1987, 1993) has continued her work and has found that despite the availability of a much better social security net in Europe than that which was available in the 1920s and 1930s, the adverse psychological effects of unemployment are nevertheless essentially similar today. The following part of this chapter is based very largely on her work. She insists on the importance of good definitions of 'work' and 'employment' and distinguishes three major categories of work: (1) employment regulated by contractual arrangements; (2) employment not so regulated (the 'black' or 'hidden' economy); (3) unpaid work, such as that done for voluntary organisations, hobbies and of course housework. She comments that:

It is often assumed that the psychologically constructive aspects of work dominate in activities outside modern conditions of employment, the negative ones in employment where, it is asserted, people have lost their concern for quality, are resistant to technological change, to innovations and labour-saving devices of all kinds as well as being unwilling to do dirty work or keep 'unsocial' hours. There is much current experience to show that this is indeed often the case. As a generalisation, however, these assertions will not hold. Not all is well in the world of employment, but neither is it in the world of work outside. The housewife syndrome of boredom and depression is still a fact of life, and not to be explained by lack of work; housewives certainly welcome as a rule labour-saving devices such as washing machines which reduce the required investment of time and effort to keep a family going. Some people engaged in craft hobbies, however, reject labour-saving devices as do some employed people ... Some self-employed may well long for the relative security of the regularly employed, their circumscribed working hours and reduced responsibility. Retired people often long for the human aspects of employment. Above all, it is the growing number of the unemployed who want jobs, not just work, and not only because of their reduced standard of living.

The last point is the most important. The deprivation of poverty is indeed severe albeit that the *absolute* deprivation of the 1930s was worse than the deprivation of the 1980s. Nevertheless, the psychological consequences of unemployment give rise to social tensions and hidden costs which are no less severe. Most of these hidden costs cannot be expressed in monetary terms, but they affect in their consequences the entire economy. The heaviest burden falls on the unemployed individuals. A voluminous research literature exists documenting the burden imposed on them. For all of them it means an enforced radical change in their way of living; for most it implies considerable financial strain; for a very large number it means sliding into poverty. It should be remembered that a high proportion of unemployed people receive neither unemployment benefit nor social assistance but are dependent on family and private support. According to some estimates this proportion is over half in some European countries (Holland, 1993, p. 124).

As already stressed however, the financial stress is not the only burden imposed on the unemployed. Even where public support is relatively generous as, for example, in the Netherlands, or where private financial resources are available as much as for the majority of the unemployed who are totally dependent on the public purse, the loss of a job has additional consequences which clearly indicate that employment means not only earning a living. The unemployed describe these consequences variously as boredom, social isolation, being on the scrapheap, socially useless, frustrated and forced into idleness. A summary of results from well over 100 studies conveyed the consensus among investigators about unemployment in the 1970s and 1980s:

In all cases the evidence suggests that groups of the unemployed have higher mean levels of experienced strain and negative feelings, and lower mean levels of happiness, present life satisfaction, experience of pleasure and positive feelings than comparable employed people. Where there is longitudinal evidence groups who became employed during the course of the studies exhibit means which improve compared with continuously unemployed groups. (Fryer and Payne, 1986, p. 247)

These psychological consequences vary, of course, from individual to individual, just as the financial burden, but not necessarily parallel to it. Where demoralisation is pronounced it stops being an individual's problem and affects the family, intensifying existing tensions between husband, wife, parents and children.

Financial and psychological deprivation combine in many cases to affect physical health. Warr (1983), for example, reported that between 25 and 30 per cent in a number of studies said that their health had got worse since they lost their jobs. Other studies found a disproportionally high number of unemployed people committing suicide and an even higher proportion among parasuicides. These studies, however, leave open the question whether unemployment caused or was caused by physical and mental ill health. There are certainly cases of either type. But in mass unemployment where whole firms or even entire industries collapse both the healthy and the sick become unemployed. One remarkable study (Beale and Nethercott, 1986) clearly showed unemployment as a causative factor. Beale, a general practitioner, had health records of workers for a period of eight years. Redundancy threats appeared after four years, large-scale unemployment in the last two years when a factory closed down. The consultation rate at his practice from the unemployed and their families rose by 20 per cent; and so did the number of attendances at hospital outpatients departments, compared to an employed control group, once the threat of redundancy had appeared. On a much larger scale Brenner's well-known studies in several countries correlated indicators of boom or recession after a time lag with national rates of morbidity, mortality and social pathology (homicide, suicide, alcoholism, etc.) and found them all higher in periods of high unemployment (Brenner, e.g. 1987).

There are, it should be noted, at least two types of people who do not personally suffer when unemployed. One group feels liberated from unsatisfactory jobs, free to engage in voluntary activities for worthwhile causes, studies or their hobbies, even if it means adapting to a low standard of living. Insignificant in numbers they are none the less worth taking note of, not only because they too are a burden on public money, but also because of what their attitudes to employment imply about working conditions.

The other type are mostly school leavers who have never had a job, though they may have had a training course to acquire better qualifications but have become cynical when there was no job at the end of it. As long as they receive support for basic needs within the family their material situation is tolerable, improved by occasional black work and scrounging, if not minor criminality. Keeping company with others in the same situation counteracts isolation; joy-riding or drugs or organised hooliganism assuage boredom. Such youngsters live without goals, without a thought for their future, alienated from the larger community. It is a matter of constant comment that rates of crime and drug-taking are rising and are interconnected. These trends have now extended to Eastern Europe as well as Western Europe and North America.

This does not mean of course that unemployment is the sole cause of these increases which have been recorded in virtually all industrial countries during the 1980s and 1990s, but that there is some association can hardly be doubted. David Dickinson (1994) has demonstrated this association in the case of Britain (Figure 1.1) for young males under 25 years of age during the 1980s, while Kirby (1994), the crime correspondent of *The Independent*, reported a survey of nearly four hundred studies in various countries, which showed that the single most effective way to reduce crime was to increase employment.

Males under 25 years
• • • • Offenders: per 100,000, right scale
——— Unemployment: %, left scale

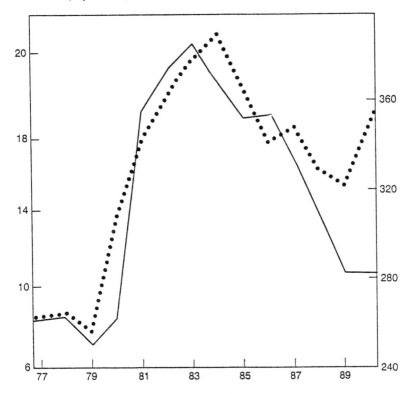

Figure 1.1 Unemployment and burglaries, Britain, 1980s
Source: Dickinson (1994).

Those few who feel liberated by unemployment are largely adults who have lost jobs which they disliked; as a rule they are well educated, committed to non-material personal goals and social values (Fryer and Payne, 1986) which previous jobs frustrated. Unemployment provides them with the opportunity to do what they consider worth doing, even at a financial sacrifice. Their way of life provides work that gives all the psychological benefits of satisfactory employment minus the money.

Both types illustrate that the psychological needs normally met in employment are deep-seated. Without a job people try to satisfy them in other social settings as best as they can; in the case of some youngsters in a socially destructive manner. Only a very few are able and willing to find socially constructive alternatives albeit at the cost of a reduced standard of living. Admirable though such individuals are, their way of dealing with unemployment does not make a dent in the macro- and micro-economic and psychological costs of mass unemployment.

Just as Beale and Nethercott had shown that the health costs of unemployment extended beyond the actually unemployed to those threatened by redundancy, so Brenner demonstrated consequences which affect an entire society. Indeed, it is one of the tragic consequences of mass unemployment that it detracts attention in the public debate from the less visible deteriorating situation of the still employed who form, after all, some 80+ per cent of the work-force. In a labour market dominated by job insecurity, conditions of work deteriorate, promotions and training are delayed, health and safety standards relaxed — and all this accepted by a work-force made more docile by the greatest fear of all, job loss (Burchell, 1992). While the consequences of job insecurity are found among all levels of the industrial hierarchy, it is on the lower levels where they are in psychological terms particularly damaging. 'Low income and enforced deprivation of basic commodities, where they occur, have adverse mental health consequences for those at work, just as much as for the unemployed' (Whelan, 1992, p. 339).

For the higher levels, the consequences of a spell of unemployment may be long-lasting and extend into re-employment, as Fineman (1987) has shown in a sensitive qualitative study. He reports that about half of re-employed managers and professionals revealed some lasting negative effect: there was the blemish on their 'record', feelings of personal failure, less commitment to the new job. 'Security and survival dominate their concerns, achievement and status were now luxuries they could no longer afford' (p. 269). As one of them said: 'I have to keep a low profile now, which I hate. To avoid issues even when I know, from experience, that the policies are faulty ... I constantly think about the vulnerability of my job, at my age, in this recession' (p. 277). Not exactly attitudes required in managers of a dynamic economy. It is hardly surprising that (contrary to popular mythology) the widespread fear of unemployment and actual high level of unemployment are usually associated not with higher levels of labour productivity but with declining labour productivity.

Mass unemployment is an unmitigated social disaster. It leads to loss of output of goods and services; it slows down the rate of new investment and economic growth; it inflicts enormous damage on social morale as well as on the numerous individuals affected; it inflicts social costs which cannot be measured as well as those which can be measured and contribute so greatly to the huge public sector deficits in many countries; finally, it generates moods of rejection, apathy, despair and irrational aggressiveness, which are a fertile soil for authoritarianism, crime, ethnic conflicts and the erosion of democratic institutions.

Just as unemployment alone cannot be blamed for the rise in crime and drug-taking, so too it cannot be regarded as the sole cause of ethnic conflicts and the rise of fascist-type movements. But one would have to be blind indeed not to observe the connections between unemployment and these phenomena, whether in the 1930s or the 1980s and 1990s. The prevention of persistent mass unemployment is consequently not just a matter of increasing the output from the economic system. It is a question of the survival of civilised society. There are of course deep historic problems which contributed to the terrible conflicts both in former Yugoslavia and in Northern Ireland but it cannot have helped matters in either region that they suffered from persistent high levels of unemployment for decades. Yugoslavia was in fact the only East European country that had this problem.

These wider social considerations reinforce the economic arguments for solutions based on spreading work through shorter hours since part-time work can at least provide some of the psychological benefits of purposeful activity, self-respect and dignity. But they also reinforce the arguments for moving as rapidly as possible to long-term solutions based on a high level of training and skills for a higher proportion of the work-force than now seems possible. *Voluntary* part-time employment is often desirable for people whose family situation or education makes full-time work impossible. But *involuntary* part-time employment as a substitute for a full-time job may aggravate problems of poverty and provide only a partial solution. The aim should be to generate enough full-time and part-time employment for all who seek it. In Chapter 4 we discuss how far the new international competition in trade and new patterns of investment and migration may affect the attainment of these objectives. In Chapter 5 we return to the theme of the changes in work organisation and in Chapters 6 and 7 to the prospects for achieving a more hopeful scenario for the future of employment. But in Chapters 2 and 3 we first address the question of technical change as we believe this to be the crucial problem in achieving a return to full employment.

As we are both more familiar with European problems and both resident in the EU we write mainly from this perspective and our illustrative examples are often drawn from Europe and especially from Britain and the Netherlands. We discuss European problems in a wider global context but in view of the great variety of national circumstances it is impossible to do justice to this variety. Nor is it always possible to provide adequate statistical evidence for the trends which we identify and the policies that we propose. We include quite a large number of tables and figures but we are conscious that, especially when it comes to policy proposals, we are discussing trends and ideas, for which the statistical information which we would ideally like to have is often not available. In addition, events are moving so rapidly that they may easily overtake what we are saying at the time of writing (March 1994). Nevertheless, we believe that the major tendencies which we are analysing are so important and so pervasive in their world-wide influence that it is worth the risk of some obsolescence as better information becomes available.

2

RICARDO'S SURPRISE: economic theory and why the fears of technical change on the part of the labouring class conform to the correct principles of political economy

Not surprisingly, economists have been stimulated to think about unemployment and its causes mainly by periods of high unemployment and the associated social distress. We do not have reliable statistics for any country during the eighteenth and nineteenth centuries but from indirect evidence and from contemporary accounts there is little doubt that the two decades following the Napoleonic Wars were one such period in Britain and other countries experiencing the early turmoil of industrialisation. Another such period was from the late 1870s to the mid-1890s. The first period gave rise to the intense debate surrounding Ricardo's Chapter 'On machinery' in his *Principles of Political Economy and Taxation* in 1821, and ultimately to the refinement of the classical theory of employment and in the United Kingdom to the 'New Poor Law' in 1834. The second period led to an extensive reformulation of the theory, a new 'neo-classical' synthesis and a variety of new policies such as 'Labour Exchanges'.

In the twentieth century again, we have experienced two periods of very high levels of unemployment — in the 1920s and 1930s and again in the 1980s and 1990s. These periods also stimulated new analysis and policies, notably the work of Keynes (1930, 1931, 1936), of Schumpeter (1939, 1943) and of Beveridge (1931, 1944). It is not the intention here to make a complete review of the extensive contemporary and historic literature on the theory of employment and technical change. Many such reviews are available (for example, Gourvitch, 1940; Cooper and Clark, 1982; de Witt, 1990; Meyer-

Krahmer, 1992; Lundvall and Petit, 1993; Petit, 1993, Vivarelli, 1994). But it is necessary to summarise the basic ideas of the main schools of thought in order to clarify the background to our own ideas and the extent to which they depart from mainstream theory.

2.1 Pre-classical economics

The early fore-runners of economics ('mercantilists') were mainly concerned with problems of foreign trade and the currency. However, the relationship between technical change and employment was at the forefront of economic policy debate long before economics emerged as a 'science' with the appearance of Adam Smith's (1776) *Inquiry into the Nature and Causes of the Wealth of Nations*. The origins of the debate can be traced back as early as the sixteenth century when awareness of economic progress and its accompanying employment displacement started to influence mercantilist policy and gave rise to a number of mercantilist writings. These were often contradictory in nature and can be considered as indicative of the continuous unease with which many economists would later on approach the debate. 'Facilitations of Arts' was the expression used at the time to describe what we now call 'technical change' and it was generally viewed with favour. As Sir William Petty (1690) cynically observed, 'introducing the ... Facilitations of Art ... is equivalent to what men vainly hoped from Polygamy. For as much as he that can do the Work of five men by one, effects the same as begetting four adult Workmen'.

But concern over the employment displacement effect was great and often led to legislation restricting the use of machinery. One example of this was the French legislation (1686–1759) on the restriction of the production, importation and use of printed calicoes. It is estimated that some 16,000 people lost their lives in the enforcement of this regulation (Heckscher, 1935).

Similar legislation existed in other European countries, including England. In 1623, for example, the Privy Council ordered a needle machine to be broken up. Yet this legislation often conflicted with the general positive attitude towards technical innovations which mercantilist writers and policy-makers displayed. As Gourvitch (1940) points out:

Colbert, the great mercantilist minister under King Louis XIV, described the inventor of labour-saving machinery as an 'enemy of labour'; but at the same time that he decidedly opposed the introduction of such machinery into private industry, he favoured its use in government enterprises 'to shorten the time and save the expense'.

These seemingly contradictory aspects of technical change meant that the employment implications became a crucial point of debate in many economic writings. On the one hand the mercantilists could well perceive the national and local advantages of technical leadership in a particular trade and the associated crafts, skills and machinery. On the other hand, the social dislocation attending displacement of labour was bound to be a matter of concern in an age when violent revolt could easily ensue. Such revolt, associated with machine-breaking did indeed become widespread during the Industrial Revolution.

The difficulties of reconciling these conflicting aspects of technical change are more clearly evident in the work of Adam Smith's immediate predecessor, James Steuart (1767). He gave a clear explanation of how sudden mechanisation could lead to temporary unemployment, which anticipated Ricardo's comments 50 years later. Whilst he recognised that there would be compensation effects in the long run, through employment growth in the machine-building industries and price reductions stimulating demand, he did not believe (as the classical economists later did in their acceptance of Say's Law) that markets would always clear. He therefore accepted a responsibility of government to maintain employment by a variety of interventionist measures including protection of strategic industries. In his advocacy of public works and the use of monetary and fiscal policies to sustain employment he anticipated many of the measures later advocated by Keynesians.

2.2 Classical economics

The paternalism and protection advocated by Steuart and many mercantilist writers disappeared with the triumph of the classical school and their powerful demonstration of the benefits of free trade and competition. A much harsher approach was felt to be justified by policy-makers and economists alike as they felt that there was now a 'scientific' basis for a general *laissez-faire* attitude and the belief that government intervention was very likely to be harmful.

In general it could be said that the classical economists brought clarity to the debate by pointing to the significant employment 'compensation' mechanisms resulting from the introduction of new technology, which at least in the long run would be operating in the economy at large. Whereas Steuart and others had already identified some 'compensation' mechanisms, the classical economists developed a much more systematic and logical approach to the system as a whole (Vivarelli, 1994).

It was therefore a considerable surprise to his fellow professionals when Ricardo introduced his comments on 'Machinery' in the Third Edition of his *Principles of Political Economy and Taxation*. After acknowledging the 'general good' technological improvements would bring about, 'accompanied only with that portion of inconveniences which in most cases attends the removal of capital and labour from one employment to another' (p. 387), he shocked his readers and provoked a furore of debate by granting that:

the opinion, entertained by the labouring class, that the employment of machinery is frequently detrimental to their interests, is not founded on prejudice and error, but is conformable to the correct principles of political economy. (p. 392)

As Paul David (1982) notices, Ricardo's suggestion that the introduction of labour-saving machinery might be injurious to the workers, causing unemployment when real wages could not be forced downwards, was fundamentally based on his recognition of lags and inflexibilities in the employment compensation mechanism, resulting directly from *supply-side* constraints.

The particular difficulty whose recognition Ricardo felt himself obliged to announce in 1821 was one that could arise in the transition to a more machine-intensive technique of production. If output had to be diverted from consumption purposes to the production of capital goods, the supply of commodities for consumption as wage goods would fall — to the detriment of the labouring population, at least temporarily. Once the new machines came 'on line', so to speak, the supply of wage goods gradually would be augmented, prices would fall, and labour could be reabsorbed into employment without there being a significant reduction in real wages (*Works*, 1, pp. 389–90). Economists in the developed countries no longer worry about precisely this form of transitional unemployment arising from technological progress. But it is worthwhile noticing that the potential problem of 'structural' unemployment is fundamentally a similar condition — one in which prolonged displacement of workers results from supply-side constraints rather than from insufficiency of aggregate effective demand. (p. 148)

However, at the time Ricardo felt obliged to modify his rather stark formulation and to emphasise the long-run compensation effects. In general, despite Ricardo's reservations and the recognition by both classical and (later on) neo-classical economists that 'compensation' mechanisms in the labour market were by no means instantaneous or automatic, policy-makers generally concluded from their theories that rather tough measures were necessary to oblige people to seek employment and to deter 'voluntary' unemployment. Nowhere did these ideas find harsher expression than in the English New Poor Law of 1834. Prior to industrialisation it had been the responsibility of the local parish authorities to provide 'outdoor relief' for those in acute distress. With urbanisation, industrialisation and the development of cyclical unemployment associated with capitalist industry, this 'old' Poor Law was subjected to increasing strains. Rural unemployment also increased with the Enclosures and new agricultural techniques. The drastic solution of the New Poor Law for these problems was to institute the system of 'indoor relief' in the hated workhouses with their separation of families and severe deterrent regimes.

The New Poor Law followed a long period of industrial strife in Britain associated with the intense hardships of early industrialisation and the dramatic dislocation of the lives of many agricultural and industrial workers. Not surprisingly, this often resulted in the destruction of machinery as well as other types of social, political and industrial conflict which brought Britain to the verge of social revolution.

Machine-breaking was often then and since referred to as 'Luddism' after the mythical leader of the Nottinghamshire riots in 1811 against the introduction of a new wide frame in the cottage knitting industry. It was both a protest against loss of employment and against shoddy quality of output. The organisers feared that lower quality would lead to loss of markets and further loss of employment. Their movement was actually quite well organised and had some success, despite the transportation of some of the young machine breakers, who had issued their warnings in the name of 'King Ludd' or 'Ned Ludd' of Sherwood Forest, like Robin Hood before him (Cole, 1948).

The early success of the Luddites caused great alarm. Secret Committees of Parliament were appointed and the doctrines of classical economics were increasingly invoked to justify repressive actions against both Luddism and trade unions. This was the background to Ricardo's famous chapter on 'Machinery'. Sporadic outbreaks of machine-breaking continued to occur in the main industrial areas of Yorkshire and Lancashire but they became less and less significant as the workers resorted in the 1830s more to strike action and to the political struggles which led to the Chartist movement for parliamentary reform and universal suffrage.

Most of the classical economists, with the later exceptions of John Stuart Mill and Marx, were worried by what they took to be an illogical and unnecessary weakening of the classical position by Ricardo. In its main propositions the classical doctrine of *laissez-faire* undoubtedly led to a tougher line on unemployment than that of earlier economists. Nassau Senior was, together with Chadwick, one of the main architects of the New Poor Law (1834) and *laissez-faire* doctrine was often (if sometimes unjustifiably) invoked to oppose even the mildest of social reforms, such as the legislation protecting children and limiting their hours of work. As Dickens and other writers showed so brilliantly, even if it was unfair to describe economics in Carlyle's words as 'The Dismal Science' it certainly had this reputation and was widely believed to justify the view that the unemployed and the poor had themselves to blame for their own poverty.

For the classical economists, from Smith to Ricardo, John Stuart Mill and most of all Marx, technical progress was one of the crucial variables in the economic system. Marx (1848) in particular emphasised the social transformation brought about by 'technological revolutions'. Thus gunpowder had put an end to knightdom; the compass had opened world markets and printing had brought about the renaissance of science. Capitalism was characterised by a restless search for new products and processes of production.

Constant revolutionising of production, uninterrupted disturbance of all social conditions, everlasting uncertainty and agitation distinguish the bourgeois epoch from all earlier ones ...
The bourgeoisie has through its exploitation of the world market given a cosmopolitan character to production and consumption in every country ...
All old-established national industries have been destroyed or are daily being destroyed. They are dislodged by new industries, whose introduction becomes a life and death question ...
The bourgeoisie by the rapid improvement of all instruments of production, by the immensely facilitated means of communication, draws all, even the most barbarian, nations into civilisation ... It compels all nations on pain of extinction, to adopt the bourgeois mode of production, it compels them to introduce what it calls civilisation into their midst, i.e. to become bourgeois themselves. In a word, it creates a world after its own image. (p. 224)

There is also little doubt that, as much in their awareness of the 'suddenness' of technological progress as in their recognition of the possibility of — at least temporarily — 'technological' unemployment, most classical economic writers simply reflected the acute conditions of the time: the dramatic technological transformations and the distressful labour conditions particularly in the period from 1815 to 1850. With the rapid growth of most economies during the second half of the nineteenth century the large-scale migration to America and the *belle époque* before the First World War, technological progress came to be regarded as gradual and continuous rather than revolutionary. As a consequence, economists' perception of the problem of technological progress and employment displacement changed quite fundamentally. As Gourvitch (1940) points out: 'As far as economic literature was concerned, the problem of technological unemployment virtually ceased to exist; it did not reappear until the 1920s' (p. 8).

2.3 The neo-classical school

Although far less severe than in the 1820s and 1830s (or the 1930s) and ameliorated by large-scale international migration, the problems of unemployment in the 1880s and 1890s were serious enough to stimulate new thinking about policies for the labour market and about employment more generally. This led in particular to the recognition that rigidities in the labour market could often be eased by the provision of better information and training for job-seekers. Legislation to introduce labour exchanges, provide elementary social insurance and improve education (Fox and Guagnini, 1993) was widely adopted in the period from 1870 to 1914, when neo-classical economics was born and became a sophisticated tool of analysis.

Summing up the attitude of economists towards unemployment before the First World War, Beveridge (1931) pointed primarily to the imperfections in the labour market as diagnosed by the British Poor Law Commission in 1909:

Now when before the war the Poor Law Commission and others studied the methods by which men found jobs, they came at once across a striking difference between labour and everything else that is bought and sold. The finding of jobs is the marketing of labour. But whereas for everything else that has to be bought and sold — wheat or cattle or tea or cotton or stocks — there had for centuries been regular common market-places, to bring buyers and sellers easily and quickly together, for labour, in this country, there had till twenty years ago been no such development. For labour there were no market-places. When the Poor Law Commission studied the matter, the normal way of hiring men was to wait for them to come to the factory gates. The marketing of labour meant the hawking of it from door to door, as many other goods used to be hawked in the Middle Ages. That persistence of medieval methods into modern times is the disorganisation of the labour market, the fourth and, in the view of the Poor Law Commission, the worst of the pre-war causes of unemployment.

That is disorganisation of the labour market in general terms. It can be illustrated by a few special cases. One such case was that men out of work in one district would set out to tramp the country in search of work, tramp blindly, often in the wrong direction. In a country with a post office, telephones, and a railway system this was clearly absurd. Another special case was the misdirection of juvenile labour; leaving boys and girls to hawk their labour with the rest meant leaving them to choose careers almost by chance, to choose careers often for which they were personally unsuited, or to enter trades which had no future at all.

Yet another case of disorganisation was the practice of casual employment, typified by labour in the docks, though not confined to it. (p. 18–19)

However, although recognising these problems of imperfection in the labour market, neo-classical economics tended to sweep away the difficulties which had worried pre-classical and some classical economists. In classical economics, technological unemployment could arise because the market could fail to absorb fully the increased production resulting from technical change and because capital supply could be insufficient to absorb the displaced labour. In neo-classical economics, the market price mechanism will take care of both.

Say's Law was fully accepted and indeed became the corner-stone of neo-classical economics from Jevons, Marshall, Walras and onwards. Whereas overproduction of particular commodities may occur, this will be accompanied by underproduction in other commodities. As Gourvitch puts it: 'There can be no general overproduction of commodities, no general oversupply of all commodities in relation to a given system of prices' (p. 87). In relation to capital supply, the possibility of the pace of technological change 'outrunning' capital accumulation is ruled out through the possibility of factor substitution between capital and labour mediated by the factor price mechanism; the wage and interest rate regulate the system, assuring that no factor of production remains 'unemployed' in the long run. Factor substitution is the main feature distinguishing neo-classical from classical economic thinking. According to Marshall (1890) 'the principle of substitution' will bring about the best possible combination of capital and labour, i.e. that in which both labour and capital obtain the greatest marginal return:

As far as the knowledge and business enterprise of the producers reach, they in each case choose those factors of production which are best for their purpose; the sum of the supply prices of those factors which are used is, as a rule, less than the sum of the supply prices of any other set of factors which could be substituted for them: and whenever it appears to the producers that this is not the case, they will, as a rule, set to work to substitute the less expensive method. (p. 536)

Furthermore, if there is excess of any one production factor, it can always be used to produce something if the correct set of prices prevails, and as it is assumed that overproduction cannot occur, unemployment cannot occur. Just as a balance of supply and demand will be secured in the commodity market through the price mechanism, so will the prices of labour and capital secure the balance of supply and demand for labour and capital. In other words, unemployment cannot occur in the long run, because there will always be a wage rate which will clear the labour market. In von Mises' (1936) words:

Lack of wages would be a better term than lack of employment, for what the unemployed person misses is not work but the remuneration of work. The point is not that the 'unemployed' cannot find work, but that they are not willing to work at the wages they can get in the labour market for the particular work they are able and willing to perform. (p. 485)

On the capital side, capital accumulation will bring about a decline in the interest rate, and substitution of capital for labour. As additional quantities of capital are substituted for labour, they will, however, be substituted in a less and less profitable way. In other words, the marginal productivity of capital will be declining. At the same time the fall in the interest rate which initially has stimulated investment demand will reduce savings, i.e. the supply of capital will be reduced, until the price of capital, the interest rate, restores the balance between the demand and supply of capital.

This neo-classical general equilibrium framework can be said to correspond most closely to present-day traditional economic views on technical change and employment. Technological change may indeed result in some temporary unemployment, but with efficiently operating labour and capital markets there is no basic economic problem arising from the introduction of new technology. It should be noted, however, that some of the leading contributors to neo-classical general equilibrium theory have expressed serious doubts about some fundamental features of the model (see Dosi *et al.* 1988, Ormerod, 1994). For example, Kenneth Arrow (1994) states:

The core of standard economic analysis and a major basis for its numerous applications in the world of policy is the theory of general competitive equilibrium (GCE) ...
GCE has served better than might be thought despite so much abstraction from the real world ...
But a long list of empirical failures mark the application of GCE. Some are literal falsifications of the model; some are omissions, important aspects of the economy which the theory does not address; and some are questions about the theory's presuppositions. I list only a few.
The best-known falsification is the recurrent and now chronic existence of mass unemployment, which is a straightforward contradiction of equilibrium. (p. 2)

However, for most neo-classical theorists, GCE still rules. Technological change is seldom viewed as 'sudden' or revolutionary, but rather the introduction of new technology and its diffusion is seen as a slow and gradual process. Even confronted with major market rigidities, the ensuing unemployment will not have anything to do with technological change. Even in cases of so-called 'biased' labour-saving or capital-saving technical change, this will have been 'induced' by changes in relative prices, stimulating both the research and discovery of new production methods and the application of technologies which might have been profitable before the relative price change, but were not used. These points lend further support to the neo-classical argument that the main causes of structural unemployment are either the failure of wages to adjust to the labour market clearing price or alternatively the decline in the marginal productivity of labour in the case of labour-saving technical change. This framework still leaves room for active policies designed to improve the efficiency of the labour market both in relation to information and mobility, as we have seen in the comments of Beveridge.

In the period leading up to the First World War this analysis did not seem wholly unrealistic but in the inter-war period with much higher levels of unemployment in many countries it was increasingly challenged on the one hand by Keynes and on the other by a somewhat heterogeneous group of economists whom we loosely designate as 'structuralists'.

2.4 The Keynesian school

Keynes was appalled at what he regarded as the complacent attitude of many of his fellow economists towards unemployment in Britain in the inter-war period. Unemployment seldom fell below 10 per cent of the labour force and Keynes (1923) remarked caustically: 'Economists set themselves too easy a task if in tempestuous seasons they can only tell us that when the storm is long past the ocean is flat again' (p. 65). The Keynesian school can probably best be distinguished from the neo-classical school by its rejection of the notion that equilibrium necessarily implies full employment. Whereas Say's Law does indeed hold in the case of full employment, it does not in any equilibrium position with 'underemployment'. These are truly equilibrium positions in the sense that they do not automatically lead to any movements which would bring about full employment. Such positions are characterised by insufficiency of effective demand. It is not the place here to go into a detailed description of the main contributions of Keynesian thinking in the area of macro-economics. Suffice it to say that Keynes denied both interest and wages the self-regulating equilibrium functions assumed in neo-classical economics.

Thus rather than increasing the demand for labour, a reduction of money-wages in the case of 'demand-deficient', cyclical — today often referred to as 'Keynesian' — unemployment will reduce further effective demand, exacerbating the unemployment problem rather than solving it. Although bitterly opposed by more orthodox neo-classical economists in the 1930s, Keynesian ideas achieved a remarkable success in the 1940s and dominated policy-making for a quarter of a century. Undoubtedly this success owed a great deal to the experience of the Second World War and Keynes' own personal success as architect of the British war economy under the Churchill government. To blame Keynes for inflationary policies is utterly absurd to anyone familiar with his life and with his work. He was as adept in devising ingenious counter-inflationary policies in boom periods as he was in developing counter-measures against unemployment during depressions. He had realised immediately in 1939 that despite the still high level of unemployment there was a serious threat of rapid inflation, as in the First World War, because of the huge scale of future military demand. Even before the outbreak of war he had recognised the inflationary pressures associated with rearmament. As a result of his timely advocacy and his brilliant ingenuity, inflation in Britain was contained from 1939 to 1945 far below the levels of the First World War.

It is often said that Keynes was deeply rooted in the neo-classical tradition of economics, and this is no doubt true. Nevertheless, even in his earliest writings it is possible to trace his awareness of the limitations of the self-regulating market mechanisms. Moggridge points out that already in 1913 in his book on *Indian Currency and Finance* he insisted on 'the essential fragility of the economic order which others took to be natural and automatic and emphasized the need for conscious management'. He cites the following passage:

The time may not be far distant when Europe ... will find it possible to regulate her standard of value on a more rational and stable basis. It is not likely that we shall leave permanently the most intimate adjustments of our economic organism at the mercy of a lucky prospector, a new chemical process, or a change of ideas in Asia.

This already foreshadows his more general onslaught on *laissez-faire* in the 1920s (Keynes, 1931):

The world is *not* so governed from above that private and social interest always coincide. It is *not* so managed here below that in practice they coincide. It is *not* a correct deduction from the Principles of Economics that enlightened self-interest generally *is* enlightened; more often individuals seeking separately to promote their ends are too ignorant or too weak to attain even these.

In 1934 his broadcast was even more explicit (see Eatwell/BBC, 1982):

On the one side are those who believe that the existing economic system is, in the long run, a self-adjusting mechanism, though with creaks and groans and jerks and interrupted by the time lags, outside interference and mistakes ... on the other side of the gulf are those who reject the idea that the existing economic system is, in any significant sense, self-adjusting ... The strength of the self-adjusting school depends on its having behind it almost the whole body of organised economic thinking and doctrine of the last hundred years. This is a formidable power ... For it lies behind the education and the habitual modes of thought, not only of economists, but of bankers and businessmen and civil servants and politicians of all parties ... thus if the heretics on the other side of the gulf are to demolish the forces of 19th century orthodoxy ... they must attack them in their citadel. No successful attack has yet been made ... I range myself with the heretics.

This broadcast foreshadowed the publication of his *General Theory of Employment, Interest and Money* in 1936, which at least temporarily was indeed a fairly successful attack on the 'citadel', and which argued that 'the duty of ordering the current volume of investment cannot safely be left in private hands' and advocated the 'socialisation of investment'. By this he meant, of course, not public ownership or socialism, but public responsibility for the overall level of investment and employment. He insisted that if private decisions to invest were inadequate to overcome a depression, then it was the responsibility of government to compensate for this deficiency. Interest rate policy probably would not be in itself a sufficient inducement to stimulate the necessary flow.

An inadequate level of private investment might arise from many causes: Keynes stressed the impossibility of purely rational calculations about the future rate of return from the new investment and the importance of a climate of confidence and the role of 'animal spirits'. He pointed to the problem of excess capacity even in some industries which had grown rapidly in the previous boom, and the problem of temporary saturation of particular markets. He stressed ironically the good fortune of Ancient Egypt in having pyramids and large-scale investment which did not 'stale with abundance' and of the Middle Ages in having cathedrals: 'Two pyramids, two Masses for the dead are twice as good as one, but not so two railways from London to York.'

Yet, in the *General Theory* he did not look at the question of investment directed towards the more rapid and effective introduction of *new* technologies, which is perhaps a more effective stimulus to 'animal spirits' than all the wonders of Ancient Egypt or medieval Europe. Since he rejected the orthodox notion that a reduction in wages would stimulate a recovery from depression, it is surprising that he did not take up the role of new technologies in raising the Marginal Efficiency of Capital. This is all the more astonishing, in view of the fact that he had clearly made the link with Schumpeterian theory six years earlier in his *Treatise on Money* (1930). He said:

In the case of fixed capital, it is easy to understand why fluctuations should occur in the rate of investment. Entrepreneurs are induced to embark on the production of fixed capital or deterred from doing so by their expectations of the profit to be made. Apart from the many minor reasons why these should fluctuate in a changing world, Professor Schumpeter's explanation of the major movements may be unreservedly accepted. He points to:
'The innovations made from time to time by the relatively small numbers of exceptionally energetic businessmen — their practical application of scientific discoveries and mechanical inventions, their development of new forms of industrial and commercial organisation, their introduction of unfamiliar products, their conquests of new markets, exploitation of new resources, shifting of trade routes, and the like. Changes of this sort, when made on a large scale, alter the data on which the mass of routine businessmen have based their plans. But when a few highly endowed individuals have achieved their success, their example makes the way

easier for a crowd of imitators. So, once started, a wave of innovation gains momentum'.

It is only necessary to add to this that the pace at which the innovating entrepreneurs will be able to carry their projects into execution at a cost in interest which is not deterrent to them will depend on the degree of complaisance of those responsible for the banking system. Thus while the stimulus to a credit inflation comes from outside the banking system, it remains a monetary phenomenon in the sense that it only occurs if the monetary machine is allowed to respond to the stimulus. (*Treatise on Money*, vol. 2, pp. 85–6)

This passage is remarkable for its unequivocal acceptance of Schumpeter's explanation of the major surges of investment in capitalist societies. It is all the more surprising that neither Keynes nor the Keynesians followed up this recognition of the crucial role of technical innovation. In fact, in the *General Theory* Keynes regressed to a position of neglect of technology when he introduced the largely artificial concept of a secular decline in the marginal efficiency of capital wholly unrelated to the actual changes in techniques or in the capital stock. Schumpeter (1952) was therefore justified in one of the main points of his critique of the *General Theory*:

it limits applicability of this analysis to a few years at most — perhaps the duration of the '40 months cycle' — and in terms of phenomena, to the factors that *would* govern the greater or the smaller utilisation of an industrial apparatus *if* the latter remains unchanged. *All* the phenomena incident to the creation and change in this apparatus, that is to say, the phenomena that dominate the capitalist process are thus excluded from consideration. (p. 283)

For the Keynesians it became a matter of relative indifference as to *which* were the new technologies and the fast-growing industries.

2.5 The structuralists

Under this heading we will focus mainly on Schumpeter and Kondratieff. In contrast to Keynes and neo-classical economic thinking, technological progress was for Schumpeter, probably more than any other economist, at the centre of the dynamics of the economic system. Whereas in the previous two schools of thought growth was simply accompanied by the emergence of new industries and technologies, for Schumpeter the system was driven by such technical innovations and their diffusion.

Schumpeter justified on three grounds his view that the process of innovation was a major source of disequilibrium in the economic system, rather than a smooth and incessant type of transformation. First, he argued that innovations are not at any time distributed randomly over the whole economy, but tend to concentrate in certain key sectors and their immediate environment, so that they are by their very nature lopsided and disharmonious and very often give rise to problems of structural adjustment between different sectors of any growing economy. Secondly, he argued that the process of diffusion, through which innovations bring about major surges of investment and of output growth was itself inherently an uneven process with cyclical characteristics. Whereas the introduction of any new product is often characterised by a slow and hesitant first start or a series of false starts whilst teething troubles are overcome, this is usually followed by a rapid growth phase. In Schumpeter's analysis this phase of very rapid growth was associated with the 'swarming' or 'band-wagon' effects of imitation, as a crowd of firms attempted to exploit the new opportunities for profitable investments and market growth, which are now widely perceived.

Finally, Schumpeter stressed that profit expectations would change during the period of rapid growth, because the swarming process would tend to erode the profit margins of the innovators. As new capacity was expanded, at some point growth would begin to slow down. Market saturation and the tendency of technical advance to approach limits, as well as competition and pressure on costs of inputs would all tend to reduce profitability and with it the attractions of further investment. Sometimes this whole growth cycle might take only a few years, but for some very important new products and technologies it might take several decades. Schumpeter maintained that these characteristics of innovations and their diffusion were sufficient to bring about major disturbances — 'gales of creative destruction' — in the economy.

With regard to employment, Schumpeter ascribed to these major technological transformations the widespread emergence of 'cyclical' technological unemployment:

(Economists) have a habit of distinguishing between, and contrasting, cyclical and technological unemployment. But it follows from our model that, basically, cyclical unemployment is technological unemployment ... Technological unemployment ... is of the essence of our process and, linking up as it does with innovation, is cyclical by nature. We have seen, in fact, in our historical survey, that periods of prolonged supernormal unemployment coincide with the periods in which the results of inventions are spreading over the system and in which reaction to them by the system is dominating the business situation, as for instance, in the twenties and in the eighties of the nineteenth Century.

Schumpeter's reference to the 1820s and 1880s indicates that with respect to unemployment he put the main emphasis on the so-called long (half-century) cycles, which he designated as 'Kondratieff cycles' after the Russian economist who described and analysed them in the 1920s when he was the head of an Economic Research Institute in Moscow. They might more properly be described as 'van Gelderen cycles' since van Gelderen had already written about them in 1913 but his work was not known either to Kondratieff or Schumpeter as he wrote in Dutch (see the first English translation of his articles by Verspagen in Freeman (ed.), 1994). Consequently, we shall continue to use the expression 'Kondratieff cycles' for the long waves which Schumpeter analysed.

The basic justification for Schumpeter's attempt to relate these long waves to technical change is that the process of diffusion of any major new technology is a matter of decades and not months or years. As Rosenberg (1976) has repeatedly pointed out, the diffusion process is seldom one of simple replication of carbon copies of a new product. It almost always involves a *cluster* of new inventions and innovations, affecting improved processes, components, subsystems, materials, and management systems, as well as the products themselves which often change out of all recognition during diffusion. The introduction of railways, of electric power, of the internal combustion engine, or of the computer are all examples of major economic and social transformations involving several entirely new industries, new types of capital goods, components, materials, new skills at all levels, new management attitudes and systems, new education and training systems, new occupational and industrial classifications, new design and development systems, new legislation and new forms of finance, company organisation, and ownership. For Schumpeter the long waves were a succession of technological transformations of the economic system. These necessitated deep structural change — a process which he called 'creative destruction' or 'successive industrial revolutions'.

Whether or not the diffusion of new technologies and the associated rapid growth of new leading sectors of the economy offers a plausible explanation of long waves in economic development depends crucially on whether some of these innovations are so large in their impact as to cause major perturbations in the entire system.

This might occur, as Kondratieff suggested, because some of them, such as railways or electric power, were so big and required such a long period for their construction that they could impart an upward thrust to the entire economy. Clearly, in addition to their own direct impact such new technologies can affect the expectations and opportunities of almost every other sector of the economy for new markets, profits, and investment. As we have seen, Keynes (1930) did once accept this Schumpeterian theory of investment. .

In principle a big upswing might also occur because of the clustering of a series of basic innovations at certain periods. Following Kondratieff's suggestion, Gerhard Mensch (1975) argued that such clustering did indeed take place during the depressions of the 1880s and 1930s, but we have maintained that the empirical evidence does not support this view (Freeman, Clark and Soete, 1982). It rather supports the notion that 'new technological systems' often have their origin several decades before their widespread adoption in the economy, not in the immediately preceding depression. Railways, steam engines, electricity, automobiles and computers were all invented and innovated long before they had any measurable effects on the wider system. The upward thrust to economic growth comes not from the first innovations, which have no perceptible macro-economic effects, but from a pattern of change associated with diffusion investment and the widespread adoption of new technological systems linking together many interrelated innovations and using a new infra-structure.

Carlota Perez (1983) has suggested that the big boom periods of expansion occur when there is a 'good match' between the new techno-economic 'paradigm' or 'style' of a long wave and the socio-institutional climate. Depressions, in her view, represent periods of mismatch between the emerging new technological paradigms (which may be already quite well advanced during the previous long wave) and the institutional framework. The widespread generalisation of the new techno-economic paradigms, not only in the carrier branches of the upswing but also in many other branches of the economy, is possible only after a period of change and adaptation of many social institutions to the special characteristics and potential of the new technology.

Pérez points out that Schumpeter did not develop any real theory of depression or of the government policies which might overcome depression. He did rather belatedly acknowledge the need for such policies in very general terms, but he adopted a generally hostile stance towards Keynesian economics. Despite his acceptance of the importance of organisational and managerial innovations and the breadth of his approach to the development of social systems, his theory of depression is narrowly economic. But it is the 'mismatch' between the institutional framework with its high degree of inertia, and the outstanding revealed cost and productivity advantages of the new technological paradigm which, according to Perez, provides the impulse to search for social and political reforms to overcome the crisis.

The structural crisis thus brought about is then, not only a process of 'creative destruction' or 'abnormal liquidation' in the economic sphere, but also in the social-institutional. In fact, the crisis forces the re-structuring of the socio-institutional framework with innovations along lines that are complementary to the newly attained technological style or best practice frontier. The final turn the structure will take, from the wide range of the possible, and the time span within which the transformation is effected to permit a new expansionary phase will, however, ultimately depend upon the interests, actions, lucidity and relative strength of the social forces at play.

In any case the time required will be considerable as institutional changes include the education and training system, the industrial relations system, managerial and corporate structures, the prevailing management styles, the capital markets and financial systems, the pattern of public, private and hybrid investments, the legal and political framework at both regional and national level, and the international framework within which trade and investment flow and technologies diffuse on a world-wide scale. To bring about such a vast institutional transformation on the requisite scale requires public policies in all these spheres. We shall discuss some of these further in Chapter 7.

From a somewhat different perspective the French 'regulation' school of economists has also stressed the need for periods of institutional change to cope with structural changes in the economy. They (e.g. Boyer, 1988 and 1993) have particularly stressed the changes in management systems, industrial relations, industrial policy and employment policy to establish a new 'regime of accumulation' appropriate to a new stage of economic and technical development.

Both they and other structural economists have emphasised that countries vary in their capacity for institutional innovation. Boyer (1989) distinguishes several different variants of 'Fordism' in Europe and North America. Sometimes, institutional change will mean 'deregulation' and sometimes 'reregulation'; sometimes it will mean the development of entirely new institutions. As Johnson and Lundvall (1992) insist, institutions do not only retard change, they can also promote change. Flexibility is needed but so are rules. They and other economists (e.g. Nelson, 1993; Foray and Freeman, 1993) have developed the concept of 'national systems of innovation' to analyse various patterns of institutional change.

2.6 Conclusions

From this brief review of pre-classical, classical, neo-classical, Keynesian and structuralist theories of technical change and employment, it is evident that all of them actually agree that the adjustment of employment to technical change is by no means an instantaneous or automatic process. Furthermore, all of them recognise that there are periods when the problems of structural adjustment and structural unemployment are particularly acute. They differ in their assessment of the speed and smoothness of the adjustment and the relative importance of the various adjustment and compensation mechanisms. At one extreme is the endogenous, self-adjusting, market-clearing model based on Say's Law, though as Keynes put it, neo-classicals mostly recognise that the adjustment takes place with many 'creaks and groans'. At the other extreme are political economy theories, such as that of Perez or Boyer, which hold that adjustment is achieved only through social and political changes to accommodate the characteristics of radically new technologies. The theories, however, are not quite so incompatible as they appear at first sight. Many neo-classical theorists would certainly accept the importance of institutional and technical change and some like Olson (1982) have themselves developed a theory of institutional rigidities. Furthermore, everyone would accept that regional disparities and the complications of trade and international competition may aggravate structural problems, as we shall see in Chapter 4. However, uncertainty about the speed of adjustment means that forecasts about future levels of employment and unemployment have varied a great deal, whether they are made by Keynesians, by neo-classicals or by others.

Contemporary forecasts of the future levels of unemployment are often pessimistic. Even those forecasts which assume a sustained recovery of production, investment, and international trade over the next few years are generally cautious about any major concomitant reduction in the prevailing high levels of unemployment. Many assume a further deterioration in the situation and even permanently higher levels of unemployment (Macrae, 1994).

Yet it seems only yesterday that almost every government in the OECD area was committed to full employment as a primary objective of government economic and social policy. Unemployment levels of 2 per cent or even 1 per cent were commonplace in most European countries (Table 1.1). At that time, in the 1950s and 1960s, it was often assumed that Keynesian theories and Keynesian policies had solved the pre-war problem of persistent large-scale unemployment permanently.

Keynes himself was not quite so optimistic about the prospects for low levels of unemployment in post-war Britain. He wrote to Beveridge (Hutchinson, 1977) that there was 'no harm in trying' to reach the level of 3 per cent unemployment, which had been adopted as a working definition of 'full employment', but with the implication that he doubted the feasibility of the target. Beveridge (1942) himself came to adopt the 3 per cent definition only at quite a late stage during the course of the Second World War. In an earlier report on social insurance he had actually assumed an average post-war level of unemployment of 8 per cent. Many other economists were far more pessimistic, and official UK government projections had at one time assumed a level of 10 per cent unemployment for a decade ahead.

Before the First World War on the other hand, as in the 1950s and 1960s, the climate of opinion in most European countries was far more optimistic. During the *belle époque* the great reforming Liberal governments in Britain adopted the commonly held belief that improvements in the flow of information, through the introduction of labour exchanges (by Winston Churchill) and other social reforms, would remove the main imperfections in the labour market. Unemployment was indeed at that time much lower than during the inter-war period.

Thus, during the course of the twentieth century we have had two long swings in the conventional wisdom about unemployment: from a relatively optimistic view at the beginning of the century to deep pessimism during the 1930s; then once more to over-optimism in the 1950s and again a deep pessimism in the 1980s and 1990s. It seems therefore that the beliefs of economists, and of the governments which they advised, were heavily influenced by the experience of the previous decade, and that their notions of the feasibility and desirability of low levels of unemployment varied accordingly. Those involved in the business of long-term forecasting will recognise this as a familiar syndrome.

Some eminent economists have explicitly assumed that growth rates will remain depressed for a long time. They frequently also did this in the 1930s and 1940s. Writing in 1981, Paul Samuelson commented:

It is my considered guess that the final quarter of the 20th Century will fall far short of the third quarter in its achieved rate of economic progress. The dark horoscope of my old teacher Joseph Schumpeter may have particular relevance here.

Samuelson's reference to Schumpeter serves to remind us that, rather than simply extrapolate from the experience of recent years, it may make more sense to try and understand the long-term fluctuations in the behaviour of the economic system. Indeed, this may help to explain the long-term changes in the opinions and theories of the economists themselves.

Great controversy still surrounds the notion of Kondratieff cycles. Many economists doubt their very existence (Solomou, 1987) and some historians adopt them only as a convenient form of periodisation. The statistical debate is likely to continue indefinitely because it is extremely difficult to reconstruct long-term time series of production, investment, employment, trade, prices and interest rates over two centuries (see Freeman, 1994).

For the purposes of the discussion which follows, it is unnecessary to adopt a position of belief or disbelief, although we ourselves believe the concept to be a useful one and the empirical evidence to be stronger than is often supposed. It is sufficient to take the agnostic pragmatic position of van der Zwan (1979) that we should endeavour to learn something from the experience of previous structural crises. In particular, we should endeavour to understand the long swings in unemployment which all industrialised countries have experienced during this century. We hope to show that these fluctuations cannot be explained in terms of conventional business cycle analysis but need to take into account additional dimensions of analysis: the rise of new technologies, the rise and decline of industries, major new infrastructural investments, changes in the international location of industries and technological leadership. It was primarily Schumpeter, Kondratieff and other long-wave theorists who introduced these topics into the debate. In the next two chapters, we shall attempt to illustrate their relevance in the case of information and communication technology. In Chapter 4 in particular, we shall attempt to show that the *international* structural changes are so great that they raise once again the nightmare of prolonged technological unemployment.

In Chapters 5, 6 and 7, we shall return to the policy debate and its relation to the various theories of unemployment which have been outlined here.

3

'THE BIGGEST TECHNOLOGICAL JUGGERNAUT THAT EVER ROLLED': Information and Communication Technology (ICT) and its employment effects

3.1 The rise of new technologies

In the previous chapter we introduced the Schumpeterian idea of successive industrial revolutions. In this chapter we shall apply this idea to the case of ICT, but first we shall illustrate the concept by the more familiar example of electrification. In his historical studies, Schumpeter (1939, 1943) emphasised the importance both of *organisational* innovations and of technical innovations, and of their interdependence. This combination is a characteristic of a change of technological paradigm, such as the introduction of information technology, and leads to changes in management structure as well as process technology.

An interesting historical analogy to the case of information technology is provided by the experience of electric power. In this case, Figure 3.1 illustrates that the major *economic* effects of electrification came over a long period with the growth in the share of electricity in mechanical drive for industry in the United States from 5 per cent in 1900 to 53 per cent in 1920. This was possible only after the acceptance of a major change in factory organisation from the old system based on one large steam engine driving a large number of shafts through a complex system of belts and pulleys, to a system based first of all on electric group drive and later on unit drive (i.e. one electric motor for each machine). Under the old system all the shafts and countershafts rotated continuously no matter how many machines were actually in use. A breakdown involved the whole factory.

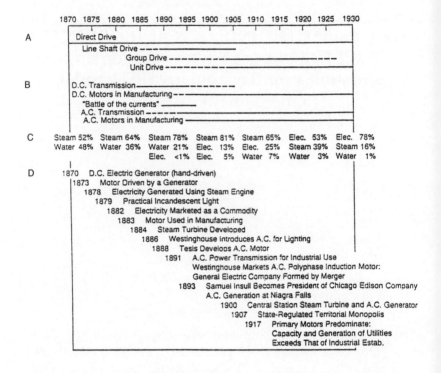

Figure 3.1 Chronology of electrification of industry:
(A) Methods of driving machinery
(B) Rise of alternating current
(C) Share of power mechanical drive provided by steam, water, electricity
(D) Key technical and entrepreneurial developments

Source: Devine (1983).

An excellent article by Warren Devine (1983) 'From shafts to wires' has documented this change in some detail. Devine points out that:

Replacing a steam engine with one or more electric motors, leaving the power distribution system unchanged, appears to have been the usual juxtaposition of the new technology upon the framework of an old one ... Shaft and belt power distribution systems were in place, and manufacturers were familiar with their problems. Turning line shafts with motors was an improvement that required modifying only the front end of the system ... As long as the electric motors were simply used in place of steam engines to turn long line shafts the shortcomings of mechanical power distribution systems remained. (p. 357)

It was not until after 1900 that manufacturers generally began to realise that indirect benefits of using unit electric drives were far greater than the direct energy-saving benefits. Unit drive gave far greater flexibility in factory layout since machines were no longer placed in line with shafts, making possible big capital savings in floor space. For example, the US Government Printing Office was able to add 40 presses in the same floor space. Unit drive meant that trolleys and overhead cranes could be used on a large scale unobstructed by shafts, counter-shafts and belts. Portable power tools increased even further the flexibility and adaptability of production systems. Factories could be made much cleaner and lighter, which was very important in industries such as textiles and printing, both for working conditions and for product quality and process efficiency. Production capacity could be expanded much more easily.

The full expansionary and employment benefits of electric power on the economy depended, therefore, not only on a few key innovations in the 1880s or on an 'electricity industry', but on the development of a new 'paradigm' or production and design philosophy. This involved the redesign of machine tools and much other production equipment. It also involved the relocation of many plants and industries, based on the new freedom conferred by electric power transmission and local generating capacity. Finally, the revolution affected not only capital goods but a whole range of consumer goods as a series of radical innovations led to the universal availability of a wide range of electric domestic appliances going far beyond the original domestic lighting systems of the 1880s. Consumer behaviour also changed, as vividly described in 'Middletown lights up' in Nye's (1990) book *Electrifying America*. Later, kitchen design had to be changed. Ultimately, therefore, the impetus to economic development from electricity affected almost the entire range of goods and services.

3.2 The rise of ICT

We would argue that, as in the case of electricity, the full economic and social benefits (including employment generation) of information technology depend on a similar process of social experimentation and learning which is still at an early stage. The organisational, social and system innovations at the point of application are just as important, or even more important than in the case of the electric power industry. Following this historical analogy, we are now able to clarify our preferred definition of ICT as a new techno-economic paradigm affecting the design, management and control of production and service systems throughout the economy, based on an interconnected set of radical innovations in electronic computers, software engineering, control systems, integrated circuits and telecommunications, which have drastically reduced the cost of storing, processing, communicating and disseminating information.

The *pervasiveness* of ICT is not just a question of a few new products or industries but of a technology which affects *every* industry and *every* service, their interrelationships and indeed the whole way of life of industrial societies. Whereas incremental changes in existing technologies cause few problems for society, a combination of radically new technologies, such as electrification or ICT, involves many social and institutional changes, some of which are painful and difficult, including of course changes in the pattern of employment and skills.

It is the reluctance of neo-classical economic theory to recognise any distinction between radical and incremental innovations which underlies its failure to come to grips with some of the problems of structural unemployment. Figure 3.2 illustrates the convergence of communication technology with computer technology. This is now the central feature of the structural changes of the 1990s. The convergence which is illustrated in Figure 3.2 looks easy on paper and in technical terms, but in terms of the real-life actors involved it is an extremely difficult and uncertain process. The old national telephone utilities and their equipment suppliers grew up with an entirely different culture and system of regulation from the younger computer and software firms with whom they must now collaborate. The culture, traditions and behaviour of both are again entirely different from the publishing, entertainment, television, cable and film companies with whom they are now forming, contemplating or breaking strategic alliances, partnerships and mergers. The boundaries of all of them are being redrawn and even more radical changes are on the horizon.

We have already mentioned George Gilder's (1993) radical vision of the future, which announces 'The death of Telephony' and of television as we know them:

Almost every feature of the telephone network, from its 4kHz wires to its circuit-switched lines, is designed for the sluggish human voice (which communicates at about 55 bits per second). Telephones give us

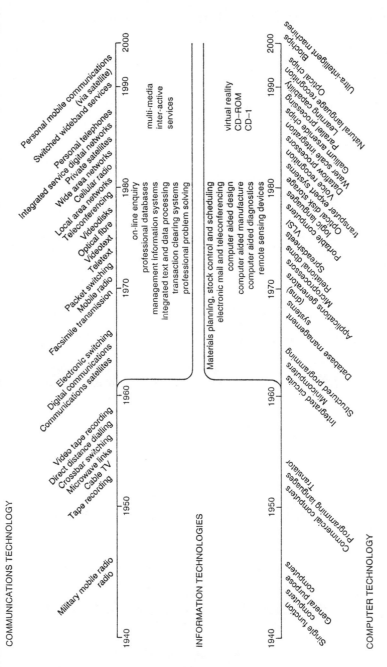

Figure 3.2 Some key events in the convergence of information technology and communications technology

dysphasics what we need: a very small bandwidth connection for a relatively long time. Computers, by contrast, need huge bandwidth for microsecond bursts. Their networks transmit digital data at a minimum rate of some 10 m bits per second, going up soon to 155m bits a second. On such a digital flood, 64 kilobits per second of voice can ride as an imperceptible trickle.

Data already comprise half of the bits in a telephone network and account for 20% of the profits. Data income is growing six times as fast as voice income. As the telephone network becomes a computer network, it will have to change root and branch. All the assumptions of telephony will have to give way. Thus telephony will die.

Television faces a similar problem. It is a broadcast analogue system which assumes that all people are essentially alike, and at any one time can be satisfied with a set of 40-50 channels. In Europe and Asia, 40 or 50 channels may seem wretched excess. But compare this array to some 14,000 magazines and a yearly output of some 55,000 trade books published in America alone. Television defies the most obvious fact about its customers: their prodigal and efflorescent diversity. It ignores the fact that people are not inherently couch potatoes; given a chance, they talk back and interact. People have little in common with one another except their prurient interests and morbid fears and anxieties. Aiming its fare at this lowest common-denominator target, television gets worse and worse year after year.

Computer networks respond to all the human characteristics that television networks defy. Computer nets permit peer-to-peer interactivity rather than top-down broadcasts. Rather than a few 'channels', computer networks offer as many potential connections as there are machines linked to the web. Rather than a system in which a few 'stations' spray images at millions of dumb terminals in real time, computer networks put the customer in control. Television will die because it affronts human nature: the drive to self-improvement and autonomy that lifted the race from the muck and offers the only promise for triumph in our current adversities.

Confidence in the new paradigm, however, does not spring only from the desire for a better culture, and it cannot be stemmed by some new global plague of passivity and tube addiction. Propelling the new order is the most powerful juggernaut in the history of technology: an impending millionfold rise in the cost-effectiveness of computers and their networks. (p. 92)

Not everyone will agree with George Gilder's effervescent speculation in *The Economist* but his piece illustrates very well the tempestuous pace of technical change and the vast uncertainties attending the future of telecommunications, television, entertainment, publishing, education, cameras, computers and software and explains why it is that telephone companies, publishers, software companies, film studios and computer companies are exploring a very wide variety of strategic options and joint ventures in Europe and Japan as well as the United States.

Nor is Gilder's vision lacking a firm technological base. He calculates that early in the next decade the equivalent of the CPUs of 16 Cray super-computers will be manufacturable on a single micro-chip which could have a billion transistors. The 4kHz telephone lines to American homes and offices will explode to a possible 25 trillion Hz of fibre optics. This type of orders of magnitude improvement in semiconductor technology, computer power and telecommunications bandwidth has in fact been achieved consistently over the past 30 years (for details, see Table 3.1) and is well within the frontier of technological feasibility.

A little more uncertainty attaches to his forecasts of the opening up of the radio frequency spectrum which he believes 'will make communication power (bandwidth) as cheap and abundant in the air as it is in wire today'. However, before dismissing his speculations as fanciful it should be noted that only a few days after his article appeared the US Federal Communications Commission adopted rules that will create three to six new wireless networks in every American city and town and the first could be working by 1996 with prices as low as half the present cellular networks (which already have over 11 million subscribers).

Table 3.1 Estimates of increase in ICT capacity

Area of change	(1) Late 1940s –early 1970s	(2) Early 1970s –mid-1990s	(3) Mid-1990s onwards: 'optimistic scenario'
OECD installed computer-base (no. of machines)	30,000 (1965)	Millions (1985)	Hundred millions (2005)
OECD full-time software personnel	>200,000 (1965)	>2,000,000 (1985)	>10,000,000 (2005)
Components per micro-electronic circuit	32 (1965)	1 mega-bit (1987)	256 mega-bit (late 1990s)
Leading representative computer: instructions per second	10_3 (1955)	10_7 (1989)	10_9 (2000)
Personal computer (PC) instructions per second	—	10_6 (1989)	10_8 (2000)
Cost: computer thousand ops. per $US	10_5 (1960s)	10_8 (1980s)	10_{10} (2005)

He accepts, however, that the digital computer networks of the future will function both over wires and in the air.

As for the descendant of television, the dominant traffic of the future will be store and forward transmission of digital data among millions of tele-computers. These machines will be capable of summoning or sending films or files, news stories and clips, courses and catalogues anywhere in the world. Whether offering 500 channels or thousands television will be irrelevant in a world without channels, where you can always order exactly what you want, when you want it, and where every terminal commands the communication power of a broadcast station today. (p. 95)

Gilder concludes that the technical changes will drive the institutional changes and in particular that centralised broadcasting stations and/or centralised telephone systems will no longer be needed, just as in his view mainframe computers will be displaced by client-server networks and networks of personal 'wallet' computers carried by most individuals.

Whether or not this vision comes about depends of course on many social and political changes, as well as on the technical changes which are in many cases easier to foresee. The social changes involve the birth of new institutions as well as the death of old ones, the rise of new forms of regulation as well as the deregulation of older services and industries. In this chapter, therefore, we consider the interplay between technical and institutional change and attempt to show that the institutional and social framework which was inherited from the past has often been ill adapted to the potential of the new technologies. This hinders the process of job generation and productivity increase. The value of exuberant visions such as those of Gilder is that they can generate the imaginative capacity to consider alternative futures.

A hundred years ago, or even fifty years ago, very few people would have imagined that most households in Western Europe would have a car, a television, a refrigerator, a washing machine and many other appliances that we now take for granted. Nor would they have imagined that the industries which produced these goods, the services which sold, repaired and delivered them and the infrastructures which they used would employ tens of millions of people.

It is comparably hard today to imagine the future patterns of manufacturing and services in fifty or a hundred years' time. Yet only with this long-term historical perspective is it possible to avoid the poverty of imagination which sees only the contemporary job-reducing side of technical change. As indicated in 2.5 and 3.1 we view the evolution of ICT as a 'change of techno-economic paradigm' (Perez, 1983) by which we mean a new technological style based on the electronic computer which affects the 'common-sense' approach of engineers and managers to the design, production and delivery of services and products. In the next section of this chapter, we shall trace the development of the new techno-economic paradigm from its early beginnings in the 1940s to the present transition period where it is becoming the dominant paradigm. These changes are summarised in Table 3.2. As in the analogous case of electricity, we attempt to show that whereas in the early period computers and other electronic products were fitted into the old organisational and institutional framework, in the 1970s and 1980s the scale of their diffusion, the reduction in their costs, the immense range of potential applications and the convergence with telecommunication technology led to the structural crisis of adjustment which we are now experiencing in the 1990s.

Finally, in the last section of this chapter, by taking the example of employment in software, we shall endeavour to show some features of the future prospects for employment as the present crisis is overcome.

3.3 Characteristics of the new techno-economic paradigm

Generally speaking, the widespread diffusion of a new technology in a market economy is possible only if it offers economic as well as technical advantages. This is why we use the expression 'techno-economic' to describe the paradigm. There are many economic advantages based on the use of ICT but the most important can be grouped under five main headings:

(1) speed and accuracy of processing and transmitting information;
(2) storage capacity for large quantities of information;
(3) flexibility in organising manufacturing, design, marketing and administration;
(4) networking within and between firms and other individuals and organisations;
(5) display of information.

The first of these characteristics — speed and accuracy in processing information — was there from the beginning of computers and telephony and was indeed the main purpose in developing computers at all from Babbage onwards.

Table 3.2 Change of techno-economic paradigm in OECD countries: a summary

(1) Late 1940s–early 1970s	(2) Early 1970s–mid-1990s	(3) Mid-1990s onwards: 'optimistic' scenario
I Information and communication technology		
Area of change **A Electronic computers**		
Early valve-based machines mainly in military applications. Future potential often underestimated. Big improvements in architecture, memory, peripherals lead to take-off in commercial market in 1950s. Huge improvements in reliability and performance from use of transistors and integrated circuits. Main-frame computers in large firm data-processing dominant but mini-computers take off in 1960s.	From 1971 the micro-processor leads to small, cheap, powerful personal computers diffusing to households as well as huge numbers of business users. These change the nature of the computer industry. Large main-frames and centralised data-processing departments play diminishing role as work-stations and PCs gain greater share of market.	Universal availability of PCs and of portable and 'wallet'-type computers linked to networks. Computers so unobtrusive in so many applications that they pass unnoticed (like electric motors in the household today). Super-computers and parallel processing for RD and other applications such as data banks where truly vast memory capacity and speed of processing are needed.
Area of change **B Computer software**		
First programming languages in 1950s. Hardware companies developing and supplying software to own standards. As applications multiply scientific users in R&D do their own software programming. Big DP departments develop software teams working with hardware suppliers. Emergence of independent software companies giving advice and support to users and designing systems.	Very rapid growth of software industry and consultancy especially in United States. Packaged user-friendly software facilitates extraordinarily rapid diffusion of computer hardware, especially to small & medium-sized enterprises, but customised software and modified packages business also grow very rapidly. Movement to Open Systems in the late 1980s facilitates interconnections and networking. Shortages of software personnel acute in 1970s and 1980s but abating in 1990s.	Reductions in requirement for software labour from (1) standard packages, (2) automation of coding and testing, (3) reduced mainframe support, (4) improved skills of users. But these trends offset by new software demand from (1) Parallel processing, (2) multi-media and virtual reality and expert systems, (3) changing configurations because of continuing organisational and technical change. Renewed surge of demand for more skilled software design and maintenance.
Area of change **C Semi-conductors and integrated circuits**		
From valves to transistors in 1950s and integrated circuits in 1960s to large-scale integration (LSI) in 1970s. Orders of magnitude improvement in reliability, speed, performance almost doubling the number of components per chip annually and drastically reducing cost.	From LSI to VLSI and wafer-scale integration. With the micro-processor from 1970s onwards, many small firms enter computer design and manufacture. Huge capacity of VLSI circuits leads to vastly increased capacity of all computers and huge reductions in cost.	Chips have become a cheap commodity. Both technical and economic limits to present stage of miniaturisation reached in early twenty-first century leading ultimately to 'Bio-chips' or other radically new nano-technology.

(1) Late 1940s–early 1970s	(2) Early 1970s–mid-1990s	(3) Mid-1990s onwards: 'optimistic' scenario
Area of change **D Telecommunications infrastructure** Electro-mechanical systems predominate in 1950s and 1960s. Traffic mainly voice traffic and telex limited by coaxial cables (plus microwave and satellite links from 1960s). Large centralised public utilities dominate the system with oligopolistic supply of telephone equipment by small ring of firms.	Massive R&D investment leads to fully electronic stored, programme-controlled switching systems, requiring less maintenance and permitting continuous adaptation to new traffic, including a wide variety of voice, data, text and images. Many new networking services develop. Optical fibres permit orders of magnitude increase in capacity and cost reduction. Breakup of old monopolies.	Widespread availability of bandwidths up to a million times that of the old 'twisted pair' in coaxial cables. 'Information Highways' using access to data banks and universal ISDN providing cheap networked services for business and households and permitting tele-commuting on an increasing scale for a wide variety of activities. Mobile phones and videophones diffusing very rapidly, linked to both wireless and wired systems.
II Industries and services		
Area of change **A Manufacturing** Mass-production industries based on cheap oil, bulk materials and petro-chemicals predominate in 1950s and 1960s boom. Electronic capital goods industries still small though very fast growing. Consumer goods (radio and TV) fit into general pattern of household consumer durables. Early CAD and CNC introduced as 'islands' of automation mainly in aerospace and promoted by government.	Electronic industries become leading edge in 1980s. Rapid diffusion of CAD, CNC and robotics in metalworking and later other industries. Productivity increases and diffusion slowed by learning problems, skill mismatches and lack of management experience. Integration of design production and marketing slow to take off. FMS and CIM have big teething troubles.	Generalisation of electronic-based equipment and control in all industries. 'Systemation' of various functions within firms through CAD-CAM, etc. Flexible manufacturing systems in most industries. Larger labour and capital productivity increases in OECD countries. Layered incorporation of Third World countries in expanding world manufacturing output and trade.
Area of change **B Services** Mass-production style spreads to many service industries, especially tourism (packaged holidays, cheap air and bus travel, etc.) distribution and fast food. Rapid growth of (public) social services and of central and local government employment. Hierarchical centralised management systems in large organisations, whether government or private.	Many services become capital-intensive through introduction of computer systems, especially financial services. Service industries also begin to do R&D and more product innovation. 'Diagonalisation' of services based on capability in ICT (tourism companies into financial services and vice versa; banks into property services, etc.). Big learning problems and software failures. Word processors become universal.	Vast proliferation of networking services, producer services, consultancy and information systems. Tele-shopping, tele-banking, tele-learning, tele-consultancy, telecommuting, based on cheap universal computing and very cheap telecommunications (Fax, E-mail, videophones, mobile phones, etc.). Growth of labour-intensive craft services, 'caring' services and creative services on personal customised basis and local networks.

(1) Late 1940s–early 1970s	(2) Early 1970s–mid-1990s	(3) Mid-1990s onwards: 'optimistic' scenario
Area of change **C Scale economies, firm size and industrial structure** Increasing size of plant in many industries in 1950s, and 1960s (steel, oil, tankers, petro-chemicals). Big-scale economies facilitate growth of large firms and concentration of industry. MNCs spread investment world-wide especially in oil, automobiles and chemicals. In late 1960s and early 1970s increasing evidence of 'limits to growth' of energy-intensive mass-production style.	Production scale economies sometimes reversed but scale economies in R&D, marketing, finance, etc. still important. In 1980s and 1990s intense competition, computer systems and cultural revolution lead to 'down-sizing' of some large firms with reduction of both white- and blue-collar employment. Many new SMEs side by side with high mortality in recessions.	Continued high rate of small firm formation especially in new technology and new service areas. Some reconcentration in capital-intensive and R&D-intensive sectors, leading to world-wide oligopolies in symbiosis with myriads of small networking firms at local level. Conglomerates with complex and shifting alliances in various regions.
Area of change **D Organisation of firms** Hierarchical departmental structures with many management layers and vertical flow of information typical of large firms. Computers fit into existing structures and often into existing data-processing departments based on tabulating machines. In manufacturing computers introduced as process control instruments of existing processes or as 'islands' in existing production systems.	Cheap widespread computer terminals lead to 'cultural revolution' in firms based on decentralisation of some functions, horizontal information flows, lean production systems and networking within and between firms. Acute stress and conflict attends clash of cultures, reorganisation of production and systemation, and out-sourcing of many functions.	New flexible management style predominates. More stable employment for core personnel with networks of smaller firms and part-time workers. Greater participation of core work-force at all levels of decision-making, but some tendencies to segmentation.

III The macro-economy and employment

(1) Late 1940s–early 1970s	(2) Early 1970s–mid-1990s	(3) Mid-1990s onwards: 'optimistic' scenario
Area of change **A Economic growth and business cycles** 'Golden Age of Growth' in mass-production industries, services and systems. Rather stable Keynesian regulation of 'vertebrate' economy providing stability and confidence for investment and consumer spending. Inflationary pressures and social tensions of late 1960s and early 1970s herald structural crisis of this paradigm as it reaches limits. Bretton Woods system provides fairly stable international framework until it breaks down in early 1970s.	First structural downswing crisis of mid-1970s leads to desire to 'get back on course' (e.g. McCracken Report). Second crisis of early 1980s leads to recognition of structural problems but only in the third crisis of early 1990s is their depth and difficulty appreciated. Huge productivity potential of ICT offset by rigidities in social system. The conflict of alternative paradigms is increasingly fought out in the political sphere as governments search for solutions and public opinion tires of the invertebrate economy with its excessive turmoil and high unemployment.	Combination of technical and social change together with political reforms leads to new pattern of sustainable growth, renewed confidence for investment and new pattern of consumer spending. Changes in UN and Bretton Woods family of international economic institutions lead to stable global framework of expansion. 'Forgotten' elements of Keynes' 1940s vision restored and provide greater resources for Third World 'catching up'. A new 'vertebrate' world economy emerges.

(1) Late 1940s–early 1970s	(2) Early 1970s–mid-1990s 'optimistic' scenario	(3) Mid-1990s onwards:
Area of change **B** Employment and unemployment 'Full employment' policies rather successful based mainly on full-time adult male employment 16–65. Relatively low but rising female participation rates. Very low structural unemployment. Recessions of relatively short duration. Low levels of youth unemployment. Expanding secondary and tertiary education systems.	Structural unemployment becomes more severe with each recession. Big increase in part-time employment and in female participation. Big increase in training and retraining to change skill profile of work-force but problems remain especially for less skilled and less educated. Long-term and youth unemployment become major problems.	Economony reverts to shallow recessions with much lower levels of structural unemployment. More self-employment and more flexible part-time work and life-time education and training for both men and women. 'Active society' providing work for all who seek it. Labour-intensive craft, caring and creative occupations and services proliferate. Shorter working hours for all and greater male participation in child care and housework.

CAD = Computer-aided design
CNC = Computer numerical control (machine tools)
FMS = Flexible manufacturing systems
CIM = Computer-integrated manufacturing

Babbage was one of Newton's successors in the Lucasian Chair of Mathematics at Cambridge and was a remarkable economist as well as an outstanding mathematician. But he is best known as the inventor of the first (mechanical) computer. His book *On the Economy of Machinery and Manufactures* (1832) showed his keen awareness of the connection between accurate measurement in manufacturing and the performance of the economy. He was thoroughly familiar with a wide variety of industrial processes and dealt in an original way with the displacement of labour by machinery.

Introducing machinery was only one incomplete route to increasing productivity: the productivity of labour could be rapidly improved through greater order, precision and labour discipline. Babbage noted the convergence of technological and economic principles on topics such as velocity and copying. (Berg, 1987)

He put more emphasis on accurate instrumentation and measurement than on steam power which, he rightly observed, was at that time used only on a very small scale. He was an early advocate of profit-sharing and worker participation in decision-making to counteract fears of unemployment. However, before the advent of electronics, the mechanical technology at that time available did not permit success with a commercially viable computer. Consequently, Babbage's dream was delayed for a century and it was only in the 1940s that Zuse in Germany and other inventors in the United Kingdom and the United States developed electronic machines with great speed and storage capacity.

The other major characteristics of computer systems developed only during the diffusion process as a result of linking computer technology with telecommunication technology and numerous related and complementary innovations in software, in peripherals, in computer architecture, in components and integrated circuits, in optical fibres and in telecommunications. The characteristics which will be discussed in this chapter, some of which were foreseen by Babbage, already give a coherent pattern for a new style of management, which is in conflict with the old style based on mass production and often described as 'Fordism'. An oversimplified and schematic contrast between these two styles is shown in Table 3.3.

This is not technological determinism. Technologies are developed and diffused by human individuals and institutions; the processes of development, selection, shaping and application are *social* processes. In the OECD (and most other) contemporary economies, the selection process is heavily influenced by perceived competitive advantage, expected profitability and (intimately related to these factors) time-saving potential. It is for this reason that we prefer the expression 'techno-economic paradigm' to the more commonly used 'technological paradigm'. However, it is also true that some technological trajectories, once launched, tend to have their own momentum and to attract additional resources by virtue of past performance. Finally, both the technological system and the economic system get 'locked in' to dominant technologies once certain linkages in supply of materials, components, and sub-assemblies have been made, economies of scale realised, training systems and standards established and so forth. Consequently individuals, firms and societies are not quite so 'free' in their choice of technology as might appear at first sight (Arthur, 1988; Dosi, 1982; Perez, 1985).

In the early days of computing it was in no way a dominant technology and had to struggle for survival in a world geared to very different technologies and systems. Even well-informed industrialists,

Table 3.3 Change of techno-economic paradigm

'Fordist' old	ICT new
Energy-intensive	Information-intensive
Design and engineering in 'drawing' offices	Computer-aided designs
Sequential design and production	Concurrent engineering
Standardised	Customised
Rather stable product mix	Rapid changes in product mix
Dedicated plant and equipment	Flexible production systems
Automation	Systemation
Single firm	Networks
Hierarchical structures	Flat horizontal structures
Departmental	Integrated
Product with service	Service with products
Centralisation	Distributed intelligence
Specialised skills	Multi-skilling
Government control and sometimes ownership	Government information, co-ordination and regulation
'Planning'	'Vision'

Source: Adapted from Perez (1990).

such as T.J. Watson, the head of IBM, did not believe that there would be any large commercial market for computers (Katz and Phillips, 1982) and thought that the only demand would be for a few very large computers in government, military and scientific applications. Early computer users had great difficulties in obtaining reliable peripherals and appropriate programmes and in recruiting people with the necessary skills. However, even in these early days, computers did already demonstrate those revolutionary *technical* advantages, which enabled such far-sighted pioneers as Norbert Wiener (1949) or John Diebold (1952) to forecast their ultimate universal diffusion.

In the 1950s, the electronic industries generally were still 'fitting in', albeit somewhat uncomfortably, to the old world Fordist paradigm. Computers became part of the centralised departmental, hierarchical structures of the large firms which adopted them. Their main advantages at this stage were the time-savings in *storing and processing* of enormous volumes of information in standardised applications such as pay-roll, tax, inventories, etc. They certainly did not yet revolutionise the *organisation* of firms, for example, by making available information at all levels in all departments. Radio and television fitted in well to the old Fordist paradigm of cheap, standardised consumer durables supplied on hire-purchase to every household, like washing machines, cars or refrigerators.

Although their revolutionary *technical* potential was already clearly visible, computers were still rather expensive, user-unfriendly items of equipment. It was widely assumed that large mainframe computers in specialised data-processing departments or groups assisted by the hardware suppliers would be the normal pattern of diffusion outside scientific and military applications. IBM became by far the most profitable firm in the world industry by operating on this basis. Its own management structure differed to a relatively small extent from those of other large firms even though it spent a great deal on training and R&D and had its own strong company traditions.

Von Tunzelmann (1993) and other historians have shown that it is realistic to regard the technical change sought by firms in *process* technology as primarily *time-saving*. He takes as an example the history of technical change in the British cotton industry during the Industrial Revolution. The inventors and entrepreneurs who launched and diffused the numerous inventions and innovations in this industry in cotton spinning, weaving, bleaching, dyeing and finishing were primarily motivated by time-saving (which also led of course to both capital and labour saving). According to von Tunzelmann's account, this was in fact the main motive for the shift from the putting out system to the factory system of production. It is also one of the main motives today in the shift to flexible production systems (sometimes called 'agile' or 'nimble' systems).

Time-saving was also very important in mass-production systems as, for example, in the speed of machining metals, the introduction of flow processes in chemicals, oil, food and drink industries or the speed of transport services. Probably, however, there has never been a technology where time-saving played a more important role than ICT. The time taken to process vast quantities of information was reduced by orders of magnitude (Table 3.1). In the 1950s and 1960s new technical advances still further enhanced this extraordinary speed by even more orders of magnitude and these advances still continue. However, in later applications of computing some of the *indirect* time-saving advantages of computer technology have become equally or more important.

The 'just-in-time' system of the Japanese automobile industry was originally a purely organisational innovation and had nothing to do with computers. However, as consultants extolled its merits and it diffused in North America, Europe and Oceania, as well as Japan, its application was increasingly linked to the use of computers and to the integration of product schedules and inventory control with purchasing and subcontracting through a network of computers. The case was similar for the 'electronification' of design. This not only meant the application of CAD and big time-saving advances in what used to be the 'drawing office': it also made possible the linkage of design offices in many different locations. Large chemical engineering firms could switch the design of a chemical plant from Frankfurt to London to Singapore or Milan at will and MNCs could link their design and engineering functions in real time in several different locations through their own telecommunication networks. Computers thus contributed enormously to the reduction of lead-times for new products and processes, as well as to greater flexibility in product mix and subcontracting schedules. Deliveries to the distribution chain could also be greatly improved and savings made in inventories through computerised warehousing and inventory control systems responding rapidly even to daily changes in consumer demand. Firms such as IKEA and Benetton clearly demonstrated the great competitive advantages which could be gained in this way.

A major characteristic of the semi-conductor and computer industry from the 1960s onwards was the very rapid change in the successive generations of integrated circuits. The number of components which could be placed on one tiny chip doubled every few years until it has now reached many millions and still continues to expand. This meant that all those firms making the numerous products which used these chips were also obliged to make frequent design changes. Rapid changes in design and product mix thus became a characteristic feature of the electronic industry and they increasingly used their own technologies to meet this requirement (CAD, networks of computer terminals, integration of design, production and marketing, etc.). Speed, storage capacity, flexibility and networking thus emerged in the 1980s as strongly interrelated characteristics of the new techno-economic paradigm (Table 3.3). Organisational and technical change became inextricably connected and there were strong pressures for greater flexibility in working hours from social changes. These interacted with the potential of ICT to deliver this flexibility. We shall discuss this further in Chapter 5.

Now it was no longer a question of 'stand-alone' computers or numerically controlled machine tools or other items of equipment, or of separate data-processing departments or separate machine shops with a few CNC tools. Increasingly, it was a question not of 'islands' within an alien and quite different manufacturing system or service delivery, but of the whole organisation being tuned in to what was previously stand-alone equipment or experimental plant. Flexible manufacturing systems (FMS and 'systemation') or computer-integrated manufacturing (CIM) became the name of the game rather than the diffusion of individual items of equipment.

Numerous case studies of diffusion of robots, CNC, lasers, CAD and so forth in manufacturing or of computers and ATM in banks or of EDI (electronic data interchange) in retail firms (e.g. Fleck, 1988, 1993; Havas, 1993) testify to the systems integration problems and the site-specific problems which arose and still arise in a widening range of firms and industries. Operating and maintenance skills do not match the new equipment; management cannot cope with the interdepartmental problems, changes in structure and industrial relations; subcontractors cannot meet the new demands; the software does not run properly, interface standards do not exist, etc., etc. Only when the *users* were actively involved in technical and organisational change and in training was success achieved. Nevertheless, the minority of firms that succeed in coping with all this turbulence can reap great advantages in flexibility yielding economies of scope, better quality and image of products, customisation of design and rapid response to market changes. These problems are intensified when it comes to the interaction of entire industries with different regulatory regimes as well as different cultures.

The world-wide intensification of competition based on rapid technical and organisational change is leading to some dramatic changes in industrial structure as well as in management structure within firms. Large firms with rather top-heavy departmental and hierarchical structures faced particular difficulties. Because of rapid, easy access to information at all levels both vertically and horizontally, intermediate layers of management were often no longer necessary. The need for rapid response and greater decentralisation of responsibility within the new production and management systems also intensified this pressure towards 'down-sizing' by reducing the number of middle managers. The changes in General Motors were vividly described as a 'cultural revolution'. Even a firm like Procter and Gamble in a year of high profitability decided to eliminate 13,000 jobs in 1993. 'Thus Proctor and Gamble embraced a practice that has quietly become the daily regime at such profitable companies as General Electric Co., American Telephone and Telegraph Corp., Johnson and Johnson Inc., the Chubb group of insurance companies, Raytheon Company and many others' (*New York Herald Tribune*, 27 July 1993). A similar trend was clearly evident in Europe in 1993–94.

These cases illustrate the general problem of flexibility of large firms confronted with a period of enormous technological and organisational turbulence. Eliasson (1992) and other economists have argued that large Swedish and other large European firms are often unable to cope with the speed of change. He also argues that the experience of IBM in attempting to acquire telecommunications capability by the acquisition of Rolm demonstrates the general difficulty confronting large firms, even when they have vast R&D and also ample resources to finance acquisitions. IBM is certainly not the only large computer firm to have experienced great difficulties recently, but it does illustrate very vividly the scale of the problems of managerial and cultural change which are needed to keep pace with the changes in technology.

However, other Schumpeterian economists such as Pavitt (1986) have argued that even very large firms *are* capable of learning and changing and that they still have great advantages and scale economies. His argument is supported by Simonetti (1993) who in an examination of changes in the 'Fortune' list shows that most of the 'disappearances' are actually mergers or takeovers and that very few (only 3 per cent) actually failed. A detailed study of the electronics industry in Finland came up with strikingly similar results (Lovio, 1994). Whilst large firms are often down-sizing and small and medium-sized enterprises (SMEs) have been flourishing in some sectors of industry, there is also evidence of reconcentration in other sectors and a new wave of mergers. These somewhat contradictory trends are characteristic of a period of structural adjustment, but in any case it is clear that SMEs have become increasingly important in all OECD countries in generating new employment and in imparting greater flexibility and structural competitiveness to the economy. IBM and other large computer firms have also entered into numerous technological collaborative arrangements with smaller firms. Even in such countries as Japan and South Korea, where large conglomerates have shown great innovative initiative, and have tended to predominate in transfer of technology, the growing importance of SMEs is apparent, although often in a symbiotic networking relationship with the larger groups. For example, in its new Electronic Technology Training Centre, established in 1990, the Samsung Electronic Company in Korea has allocated 20 per cent of the training places to the 2000 SMEs with which it cooperates.

In considering the importance of small firms for employment growth and public policy it is important not to over-simplify the issues. Although many large firms have been shedding labour, this is certainly not true of all. There are firms generating new employment in every size category and many of these are to be found in the ICT industries, despite the fact that others have been sharply reducing their labour force. There is a great deal of restructuring *within* the ICT industries based on the success of personal computers, automation of many processes, micro-processors, customised chips and rapidly evolving product and service mix.

The final part of this chapter will deal with changes in the ICT industries and especially with future employment trends in software, hardware and information services. It will argue that despite the recent wave of down-sizing in large firms and despite the labour-saving techniques diffusing in software as well as hardware, there is nevertheless enormous scope for a vast process of job generation.

3.4 ICT and the growth of employment

The first three parts of this chapter have dealt with the interdependence of technical and institutional changes. The third part has attempted to show that a new style of management and a new pattern of organisation within and between firms has emerged as a result of these changes. The development and diffusion of this new pattern has been and still is a long and painful process for both large and small firms since it has involved intensified competition and the displacement or reform of many old institutions and practices. We now turn to the *creative* side of this process of creative destruction.

Despite all the turbulence and all the restructuring, the ICT industries and services have been the fastest growing group of activities in world production, world trade and world employment. They have also shown the highest rates of productivity increase both in capital productivity and in labour productivity. *Software* productivity is particularly difficult to measure. Lines of code are obviously unsuitable and much ingenuity has been used to devise new measures based on Albrecht's 'Function Points' which are independent of source code or language used. Despite the measurement problems there is growing evidence that some important breakthroughs have now been made in software productivity (Quintas, 1993; Rasch and Tosi, 1992; *Business Week*, 14 June 1993; Swanson *et al.*, 1991; Panko, 1991; Henkoff, 1991; Brynjolfsson, 1991). The contribution of computers and software to productivity in other industries has been hotly debated but the most authoritative recent study (Lichtenberg, 1993) showed exceptionally high returns to investment in computer capital.

People sometimes tend to think that employment and labour productivity move in opposite directions, i.e. a high growth rate in labour productivity would be associated with declining employment. This is sometimes true in mature or declining industries, such as mining and agriculture. However, historically, the evidence is strong that with new products and services a 'virtuous circle' of high output growth, high employment growth and high labour productivity growth tend to go together and to reinforce each other. This was the case, for example, with textiles during the industrial revolution and with steel and automobiles earlier this century. This is because the rapid diffusion of *new* products and processes is strongly associated with cost reduction and high income and price elasticities. Whilst ICT *hardware* prices have indeed been falling dramatically because of the falling cost of chips (bucking the world-wide inflationary trends), *software* costs and prices have tended to rise, thus acting as a brake on the diffusion of ICT systems. Consequently, there are good reasons to believe that rising software productivity would generate an even faster increase in software employment and not a reduction, as might appear at first sight.

Many ICT companies continued to show high growth rates throughout the recession of the early 1990s, even though some of the largest companies experienced a downturn in sales of computer hardware. No fewer than 38 of the 100 fastest growing companies in the

United States over the past five years were ICT companies (Juliussen and Juliussen, 1993). Many of them had growth rates of 50 per cent or more per annum and they included software companies, networking services, peripherals, telecommunication services, information services, disc drives and components. All of these were quoted companies with sales greater than $300m. per annum. Both in the United States and the United Kingdom the small recovery in national output and productivity which took place in 1992–3 was largely based on the computer industry and related services. Estimates of the fastest growing companies in terms of labour productivity over the past five years also show that about one-third of these companies are in the ICT industries (*Business Week*, 14 June 1993). Even though the shift from mainframes to client-server networks and to PCs and portables caused some problems for American, European and Japanese *hardware* manufacturers, the software, information systems and networking services continued to show great dynamism in the whole world economy. For a small sample of the largest firms in the world industry *Datamation* (15 June 1993) estimated that revenues of firms providing software grew by more than 150 per cent between 1988 and 1992, and information service revenues by more than 70 per cent. Sales of the Japanese information service industry grew by more than 300 per cent between 1985 and 1991 (Baba *et al.*, 1994).

We shall take the example of software employment to illustrate the general problem of assessing the future potential impact of ICT on employment growth. *Employment* in software and information services was one of the fastest growing categories in all OECD countries in the 1980s. In Japan employment grew from about 75,000 in 1980 to over 350,000 in 1990 (Baba *et al.*, 1994). In the United States the number of employees in 'computational data processing services' grew from 304,000 in 1980 to 835,000 in 1991 (*Statistical Abstract*, 1992). These official estimates understate total software employment because of the difficulties of measuring software activities in *user* firms both in the United States and in Japan.

The total number of people working in software activities of all kinds, i.e. the software industry, plus hardware firms, plus user firms is two or three times as great as the official figures for the software 'industry'. In the United States where the specialised industry is strongest, there are probably now (1994) about two million people employed in software work. In Japan there are nearly a million and in Western Europe well over two million. These estimates can be cross-checked with many consultants' reports and independent industry estimates even though there are no official figures. For example, in

Britain, whilst hardware industry and software employees with 'IT skills' were estimated at 120,000 in 1988, the number of employees with IT skills was estimated as an additional 180,000 in *user* industries and the growth rate of employment as 8 per cent per annum (Oakley, 1990). There is thus no doubt that software and information services have been one of the fastest growing categories for new employment in the past decade and that the total employment gains were much greater than those registered in the software industry itself. World-wide there were well over ten million people working in software activities by 1994.

Many estimates of future employment growth forecast a continuing high growth rate for software, although not quite so rapid as in the 1980s. Thus the US Bureau of Labor (1992) in its forecasts for the year 2005 puts the projected growth for 'computer scientists and systems analysts' as 79 per cent from 1990 to 2005 and for 'computer program-mers' as 56 per cent. No other occupations except 'home health aides' show such high growth (Table 3.4). No similar official forecasts exist for the European Union but many similar national forecasts were made in the past.

However, some well-informed commentators have cast doubts on these estimates of future employment growth in the service indus-tries, particularly for software. For the first time in the 1990s' reces-sion, there have been significant redundancies among software employees and it has been suggested that software employment has reached a plateau and might even decline in the future.

The reasons which are sometimes advanced to justify a pessimistic forecast for future software employment are these:

(i) The automation of coding and testing of new software.
(ii) The spread of Object-Oriented Programming (OOP) and other techniques which greatly increase software labour productivity.
(iii) The universal availability of standard packages, many of which are user-friendly relieving the users of the need to hire specialist software personnel.
(iv) The improved skills of software users, many of whom no longer need 'hand-holding' support. A high proportion of graduates in many different disciplines now have computer skills, even though they are not designated as software or computer professionals.
(v) Related to this, the need for mainframe data processing or spe-cialist support groups is said to be diminishing with the shift to client-server networks.
(vi) The subcontracting of some software activities to Asia and to the Caribbean (and on a small scale now to Eastern Europe).

Table 3.4 *Outlook 1990–2005:*
occupational employment forecasts for the United States

Occupations with the largest job growth, 1990–2005, moderate alternative projection ('000s)

Occupation	Employment		Change	
	1990	2005	Numerical	Per cent
Salespersons, retail	3,619	4,506	887	24.5
Registered nurses	1,727	2,494	767	44.4
Cashiers	2,633	3,318	685	26.0
General office clerks	2,737	3,407	670	24.5
Truckdrivers, light and heavy	2,362	2,979	617	26.1
General managers and top executives	3,086	3,684	598	19.4
Janitors and cleaners, including maids and housekeeping cleaners	3,007	3,562	555	18.5
Nursing aides, orderlies and attendants	1,274	1,826	552	43.4
Food counter, fountain and related workers	1,607	2,158	550	34.2
Waiters and waitresses	1,747	2,196	449	25.7
Teachers, secondary school	1,280	1,717	437	34.2
Receptionists and information clerks	900	1,322	422	46.9
Systems analysts and computer scientists	463	829	368	78.9
Food preparation workers	1,156	1,521	365	31.6
Child care workers	725	1,078	353	48.8
Gardeners and groundkeepers, except farm	874	1,222	348	39.8
Accounts and auditors	985	1,325	340	34.5
Computer programmers	565	882	317	56.1
Teachers, elementary	1,362	1,675	313	23.0
Guards	883	1,181	298	33.7

Table 3.4 continued

Occupation	Employment		Change	
	1990	2005	Numerical	Per cent
Teacher aides and educational assistants	808	1,086	278	34.4
Licensed practical nurses	644	913	269	41.9
Clerical supervisors and managers	1,218	1,481	263	21.6
Home health aides	287	550	263	91.7
Cooks, restaurant	615	872	257	41.8
Maintenance repairers, general utility	1,128	1,379	251	22.2
Secretaries, except legal and medical	3,064	3,312	248	8.1
Cooks, short order and fast food	743	989	246	33.0
Stock clerks, sales floor	1,242	1,451	209	16.8
Lawyers	587	793	206	35.1

Source: *US Bureau of Labor Statistics (1992).

If it were true that for the above reasons software employment would level off or decline in the next decade, this would be a very important change in the labour market. However, there are also some good reasons to believe that employment growth will continue at a high rate both in Europe and the United States.

The main reasons for a more optimistic forecast are the following:

(i) ICT will continue to diffuse at a very high rate over the next decade. There are still innumerable applications of computers and all of these require software for their implementation. As we have already argued, rising labour productivity in software would accelerate rather than retard diffusion, so that output and employment growth would outstrip labour productivity growth.

(ii) Even though it is perfectly true that standard software packages have vastly improved and diffused very widely, the needs, the technology and the organisation of firms are changing all the time and will continue to do so. To achieve a good 'match' between technology, organisation and software is not a matter of static 'maintenance' but a creative activity which will continue to make new demands on software skills. However, it is true that the balance of employment growth will probably shift from 'programmers' to 'systems design' or even to managers and engineers who may not be designated as 'software' people at all.

(iii) Most large organisations have inherited a mixture of hardware and software from different suppliers. PCs and portables have proliferated at the fringes and their numbers are now very great. However, the need remains for client-server networks and for many other networks based on reliable secure communication. Despite the spread of 'open systems' much effort for the foreseeable future will continue to go into 'middleware', i.e. software appropriate to organisations operating a variety of different equipment, much of which cannot simply be scrapped despite the high rate of technical change.

(iv) Parallel processing, virtual reality and multi-media are all likely to experience extraordinarily rapid growth in the next decade and all will make huge new demands on software applications skills.

(v) The small-scale redundancy which has been experienced, especially in the United Kingdom and the United States is mainly associated with temporary phenomena such as defence business contraction, switch from old programming languages, such as COBOL, to the newer programming languages such as C and to the effects of the recession.

(vi) As already indicated in the introduction to this section, there is a vast new area of potential employment growth associated with the infrastructural investment in cable and both wired and wireless telecommunications, which is taking off in the United States, Europe and Japan. This growth will be in many new interactive services to *households* as well as to business. Part of it will initially be 'edu-tainment'. Computer games have probably been the fastest growing area of ICT activities in the past few years and companies such as NINTENDO and SEGA have experienced astonishing growth even for ICT companies. This has shown that there is an enormous world-wide demand from children (and adults) for this type of product — home entertainment linking new software products with TV and PCs in an interactive mode. Some of the recent products already are on the borderline between entertainment and education (e.g. 'MARIO IS MISSING' is in some respects a geography lesson which can still rivet the attention of 10-year-olds). The demand for home education to complement the formal education system is potentially almost limitless, as is the learning capacity of most human beings. This market will be opened up by enterprising companies and educational organisations all over the world but it will require extraordinary software skills, linked to multi-media and entertainment skills. In the immediate future an *even greater* demand is being generated in the education system for CD-ROM packages offering new ways of learning in every discipline. This is discussed in detail in Chapter 7.

(vii) The international tradability of many services will increase and the characteristics of ICT will vastly enlarge the world market. This aspect is discussed in the next chapter.

It is not difficult of course to generate a far more pessimistic and cynical scenario for the future of software employment and all the related service activities. John Lippman in the *New York Herald Tribune* on 1 September 1993 in a report headed 'They've seen the Future and switched channels' described the results of an experiment in multi-media, inter-active TV in Cerritos, California as follows:

What's it like living along the information superhighway? Apparently, you don't even notice it. After four years in the multimedia fast lane, residents of this Los Angeles suburb still spend more time on the freeway than the data expressway.

It wasn't supposed to be that way. Four years ago, James L. Johnson, chairman of GTE Corp., cut a ribbon in Cerritos and proclaimed the suburb would be the site of the most sweeping test yet of interactive television, a test that would 'shape future telecommunications for the whole country'.

GTE installed what was probably America's most sophisticated cable system, permitting many subscribers to use their TV sets interactively. The project generated a flood of attention over how residents would bank and shop at home, obtain city permits, bone up for college entrance exams, play games and access movies at the flick of a button.

But after a prolonged opportunity to serve as guinea pigs for the TV of tomorrow, hardly any residents subscribe. Most do not even get cable TV, and many who do say they are not interested in ordering flowers on-line or scanning an interactive encyclopedia.

'Quite frankly, I don't know of anyone who uses it,' said Mayor John Crawley. 'For the average person in Cerritos, it doesn't exist.'

GTE officials insist they are happy with the reception for their new services, although they will not discuss how often customers use them.

GTE's project head, Done Bache, admits that the problem has been finding out what subscribers are willing to pay for the convenience of a film that appears within minutes.

'A lot of what we're doing here is speculation,' he said. 'I don't know if we can prove demand exists for all these services.' But, he added, interactive TV should parallel the deployment of other technologies, which often take years to catch on. 'You have to in some sense create the demand, like ATM machines,' he said.

That hasn't happened yet. Meanwhile, the indifference of Cerritos residents suggests that Americans are far from ready for the dawning age of interactive TV.

GTE's experiment is important because it foreshadows the much-ballyhooed era of the 500-channel, two-way cable system. The Cerritos experience suggests that if the future of telecommunications is really going to be interactive, it had better be mindlessly simple and endlessly diverting – not unlike plain old television. And it may not be nearly as big a business as some have suggested.

There could scarcely be a greater contrast with the exuberant technological optimism of George Gilder reported in Section 7.2. The results of the Cerritos experiment and similar experiments elsewhere are quite consistent with the views of those economists such as Pasinetti (1981) who have insisted that the pattern of consumer expenditure is very conservative and that a new pattern will be slow to emerge. It is certainly hard to predict. Some services, such as teletext and related services, have diffused relatively slowly; others, such as FAX, Inter-Net and computer games, with extraordinary rapidity. There were 150,000 new subscribers to Inter-Net every month in 1993. The experience of tele-working and tele-shopping has been similarly diverse. Nevertheless, the experience of 'First Direct' (a branch of the Midland Bank offering a full range of home banking services) shows conclusively that a well-designed service can be extraordinarily successful and diffuse very rapidly. As has already been shown, the overall growth rate of ICT products and services remains extremely high, despite some disappointments and failures.

These alternative views of the future of ICT and the related employment in software illustrate too the great importance of institutional change and of public policies which are discussed in Chapters 6 and 7. The speed of diffusion and the associated employment gains will undoubtedly depend heavily on economic policy more generally as well as on specific policies for institutional change in areas directly affecting ICT.

4

'GET SMARTER OR GET POORER': The
international dimension of technical change
and employment in the world economy

Many of the present fears about unemployment associated with technical change are strongly related to the increasingly international implications of *computerised* technical change. Whereas there is little doubt that there are many employment creation features associated with the emergence and further diffusion of information and communication technology, there are also good reasons to assume that such employment creation might occur increasingly in other countries far removed from the country of origin of such technologies. At the same time, and alongside a more traditional and expected pattern of relocation of unskilled manufacturing activities in low wage countries, manufacturing employment in such activities in the developed 'Northern' countries has increasingly been competed away. What adds in particular to this international relocation process in manufacturing (Wood, 1994) is the role of information and communication technology in enabling increased international tradability of a number of hitherto 'untradable' service activities. Yet it has been precisely those service activities which have until now provided most of the employment growth in the developed OECD countries. The fear of a rapid growth in unemployment associated with the further diffusion of ICT is consequently in the first instance related to the potential displacement of many routine jobs in manufacturing *and* services to lower labour cost regions and countries.

Before turning in more detail to some of those fears, we briefly review some of the international structural features of present trends in employment growth in Europe, the other OECD countries and some of the newly industrialising countries in South and East Asia, representing to some extent the 'South', although growing much more rapidly than the countries of Africa and Latin America and characterised especially by the speed with which they have adopted ICT.

4.1 Structural change and employment growth

The 1980s and 1990s have not only been the period of dramatic growth of modern information and communication technologies; they also have been a period of major structural change in the world economy. From a vision in the mid-1970s that, after the first oil shock, OECD economies would quickly return to full employment (see e.g. the so-called McCracken OECD Report, 1977), a broad consensus has emerged amongst policy-makers that various facets of 'structural change' have had and are still having a major impact on the structure of unemployment (long-term, youth, unskilled, excluded workers, etc.) and on different countries' capacities to generate new employment opportunities.

That policy-makers woke up to the importance of structural change, even in a recessive period with substantial growth in cyclical unemployment is not really surprising. The last five to ten years can indeed, and probably best be described as a period of historically major structural change. One may list the end of the cold war and the collapse of the former socialist countries; the shift in world market growth from the North Atlantic OECD area (the United States, EU, EFTA) to the Pacific basin area with new countries such as South Korea and Mexico joining now the club of OECD developed countries, and possibly others in a position to do so in the near future; the creation of regional trading blocs with a resultant much more rapid growth of trade *within* than between such integrating trade areas; the surge in foreign direct investment in these trade blocs with large firms aiming at presence in each of these markets; the growing impression of a dramatic reduction in physical distances — the world as a village — be it in terms of communications (with as typical examples financial services or world information) or the decline in the relative cost of migration.

These processes of structural change have made policy-makers, economists and businessmen much more aware of the increased international implications of their policy actions. Policies which might appear 'sustainable' within a national context might increasingly not be so in an international or regional trade bloc context. This opening up to international restructuring processes greatly accelerated in the 1980s and quickly demonstrated how freedom of policy actions in a wide variety of different fields has been reduced in most countries. Combined with the more traditional processes of structural change associated with technical change (changes in the industrial and service composition of employment, changes in demand for new commodities and services), these new features of international structural change, including North–South trade and international relocation, question increasingly the automaticities of 'employment compensation' and the employment creation capacities of high wage and high labour cost economies.

While we take as our starting point the international structural change features described above, we limit the analysis here to some of the trends in employment, both at the aggregate and disaggregate level, and in international trade and competitiveness both at the aggregate level and with respect to ICT.

4.2 Trends in employment: growth in Asia at the expense of Europe?

Figure 4.1 illustrates how employment creation capacities have varied between different OECD countries (the United States, Japan, the EU and EFTA countries) and the South and East Asian countries (SEA consisting of Hong Kong, Indonesia, Malaysia, the Philippines, Singapore, South Korea, Taiwan, Thailand) over the last 20 years. The figures for 1993 and 1994 are estimates.

The United States as technological leader and most developed country has experienced big demographic changes and a remarkable employment growth pattern, where over the last ten years some 18 million jobs have been created. Since 1960 total employment nearly doubled. Much has been written about the US pattern of employment growth. What appears from Figure 4.1 is that the popular notion in the United States of 'jobless growth' is, if anything, only a recent, not very pronounced process. The Japanese economy was also characterised by substantial employment growth over the 1980s. Despite average productivity growth rates in Japan of some 3.4 per cent a year, employment also grew at some 1.2 per cent a year. In this period, although not in the 1990s, Japan enjoyed the benefit of relatively high output growth combined with high productivity growth.

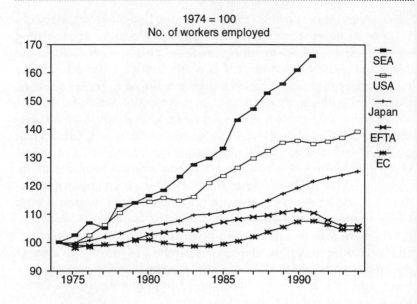

Figure 4.1 Development of employment, 1974–1994

Source: ILO, OECD statistics.

By contrast, the EU countries, and since the 1990s the EFTA countries too, have been witnessing virtually 'jobless growth' for a long time. There has barely been any net growth in employment over the last 20 years. Surprising though is the fact that the EU countries' period of most rapid employment growth occurred in the 1985–90 period. Employment grew at the historically unprecedented rate of 1.3 per cent a year, creating some nine million jobs. However, the shedding of employment in the early nineties was so large that all the gains in employment over the exceptional period 1985–90 were lost. As Figure 4.1 points out, compared to other OECD countries, European countries, both the EU and EFTA have been characterised by low net employment growth over the last two decades and negative growth in the early 1990s.

In contrast to these trends in employment growth, the South and East Asian countries have been characterised by extremely rapid employment growth, on average some 2.5 per cent a year. Whereas the United States nearly doubled its employment in 30 years, the Asian economies did so in 20 years. This rapid growth in employment has gone hand in hand with rapid output *and* productivity growth. This overall pattern of growth in output, productivity and employment, as illustrated in Figure 4.2, can be best described as a process of 'catching-up' to productivity levels and consumer demand of the Western developed countries. The catching-up process has still a long way to go, but the self-reinforcing dynamics of the process, combined with the huge concentration of world population in this area of the world, have made East and South Asia the new growth pole of the world.

As also illustrated in Figure 4.2, Japan has traditionally been the developed OECD country which compared most favourably with this successful 'catching-up' growth pattern. As we have already seen over the 1970s and 1980s Japan witnessed an impressive output growth (on average 4.5 per cent), higher than the substantial productivity growth of 3.4 per cent a year, with as a result a small but steady employment growth just above 1 per cent a year. Whether Japan will be able to resume such high, 'full employment' output growth in the 1990s given the high yen and the increased competition from other low cost-based East Asian economies, or whether it will start to resemble European unemployment levels, will depend very much on its capacity to keep ahead of other East Asian economies in benefiting from the new growth opportunities in Asia, and whether she can successfully adjust the strong industrial structure of the economy towards a more service-oriented structure.

a) Production

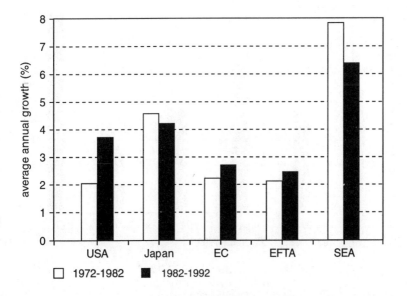

b) Employment

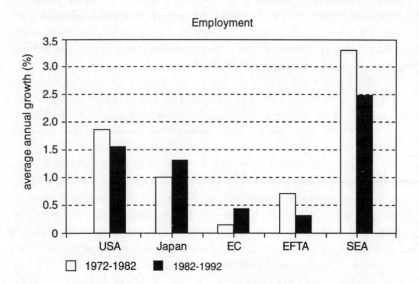

c) Productivity

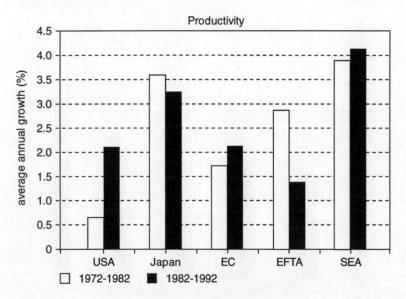

Figure 4.2 a-c Average annual growth 1972–1992 (Productivity growth = output growth per manhour)
Source: ILO (1992), OECD, CRONOS Database.

By contrast, the United States with absolute levels of productivity still higher, according to the recent McKinsey Report, in most industrial and in all service sectors than in Japan and Europe (exceptions with respect to Japan include steel, motor vehicles and consumer electronics), has witnessed a lower growth in productivity than Japan or Europe, so that most of its output growth has been accompanied by employment growth. This high 'employment intensity' of US output growth has been accompanied by employment creation in many low-skill jobs in service sectors, but also, as we shall see, in a number of high-tech service and manufacturing activities.

Finally the EU and also the EFTA countries have been witnessing relatively low output growth with nevertheless a high productivity growth (for the period 1982–92 the EU had, with the SEA countries and Japan, the highest labour productivity growth), so that employment growth has been very low. The variety of trends in employment, output or productivity growth, as summarised in Figure 4.2, hide in other words some crucial structural change features, which appear to have had a much stronger impact in some countries than in others. To draw policy conclusions from aggregate trends is thus difficult because no insight is given into the underlying structural causes for productivity growth. The latter might indeed be the result of: changes between sectors, and in particular between manufacturing and services; or even changes between occupations and skills; changes in competitiveness and in growth opportunities or whether employment is being created in old, mature industries or new, high-tech services, some of which might be internationally traded whereas others might not (yet) be, or changes in the sort of employment being created — low-wage, unskilled jobs or high-wage multi-skilled jobs. Where in the world such employment is created may matter a great deal in any debate on future employment growth.

This explains why even in countries with high employment growth such as the United States, and economies with low unemployment such as Japan, there is almost as much public debate on structural change and employment as in countries with very high unemployment such as Europe. It also explains, why, in our view, simplistic macro-economic visions about creating more employment through slowing down productivity growth — increasing e.g. the so-called 'employment intensity' of growth in the EU — will not lead the policy debate on employment growth very far. To do so requires a more in-depth look at some of the major structural changes occurring in the economy, most of which will be associated with technical change — something to which we turn next.

4.3 Sectoral shifts in employment: from manufacturing to services

In Figure 4.3 the distribution of employment in the primary, secondary and tertiary sectors for the OECD countries and the same East and South Asian industrialising countries as in Figure 4.1 are represented. The data for the OECD countries illustrate the general shift away from agriculture and industry into services. The service sector accounts now for between 60 and 70 per cent of total employment in most OECD countries. Accompanying this steady increase in service employment share, both the United States and Europe have witnessed a steady decline in their manufacturing employment share. By June 1993 no more than 18 per cent of the total US labour force was still employed in manufacturing.

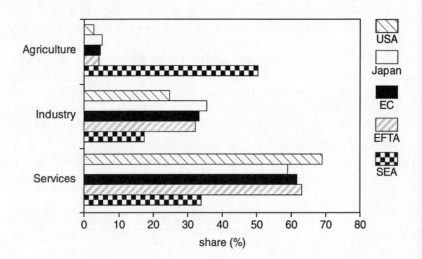

Figure 4.3 Sectoral employment shares, 1990

Source: ILO (1992).

But the contrast between the OECD and the East and South Asian economies relates in the first instance to the size of the agriculture sector. Whereas all countries saw their share of employment in agriculture decline the difference between the absolute levels remains striking, with, however, substantial variation between both the OECD and Asian economies. Turkey, Greece, and to a lesser extent Portugal, resemble much more the developing economy pattern than Hong Kong, Singapore, Taiwan or South Korea. In industry the picture looks less strikingly different between the OECD and Asian economies. All OECD countries, with the exception of Turkey, have seen their employment share in industry decline and this is also now the case for East Asia. However, the decline in manufacturing employment has been smallest in Japan and the Southern 'industrialising' European countries, Portugal, Spain and Greece. By contrast Indonesia, Malaysia and the Philippines still saw their industrial employment share rise.

With respect to services it is obvious that this sector is now by far the dominant employment provider in most developed countries. However, as Figure 4.4 illustrates, the growth in the employment share of services is in no way confined to the OECD area. As a matter of fact the growth in the service employment share has been more rapid in the most recent period in South and East Asian economies than in the United States or Japan, illustrating again that the catching-up process in these countries also includes a structural shift towards service activities.

The complexity of these trends should not be disregarded. Part of the decline in 'manufacturing' employment is due simply to the sub-

a) Agriculture

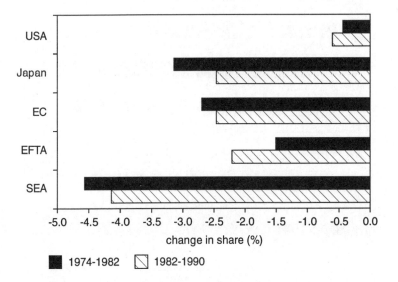

b) Industry

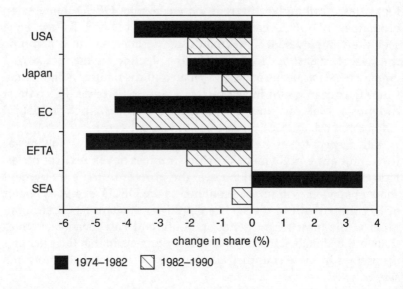

c) Services

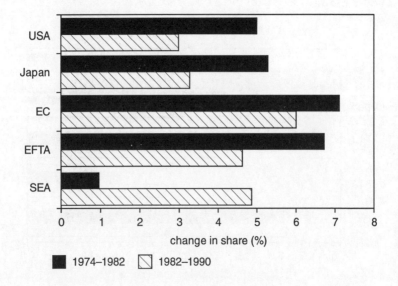

Figure 4.4 a-c Change in employment shares, 1974-1990

Source: ILO (1992).

contracting of activities which were until recently performed 'in-house', i.e. *within* manufacturing. A 'post-industrial' society will certainly not be one without manufacturing, any more than an industrial society is without agriculture, but the numbers employed may be much smaller. Moreover, many service and manufacturing activities are highly interdependent and these broad structural shifts are to some extent typical of economic development. They illustrate nevertheless the significance of the structural 'transitions' occurring during any process of growth. Behind growth one observes in other words continuous shifts in employment growth between sectors, caused by the complex interplay between technology and demand. Technology will indeed lead to efficiency improvements in production, e.g. in agriculture and industry, resulting in declines in employment, if growth in output does not compensate sufficiently for such productivity gains. Whether it does so will depend on price and income elasticities — the most well-known cases where such compensating effects will be insufficient relate to food and basic commodities. Engel's law postulates a declining proportion of rising income is spent on food and the steady long-term decline in agricultural employment is due to the combined effect of technical change and this law.

Similar changes, induced by changes in technology and demand, are of course occurring at a more disaggregated level, *between* industrial sectors. At the level of the United States, Japan and the EU, Figure 4.5 illustrates the changes in industrial employment in the

a) United States

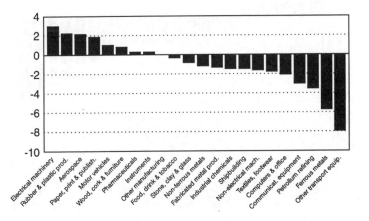

b) Japan

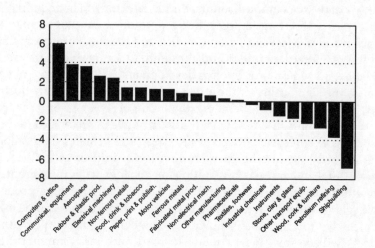

c) European Union

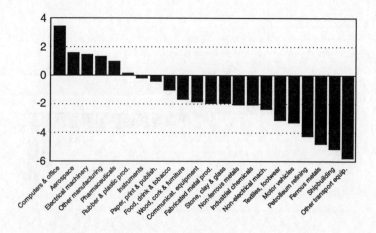

Figure 4.5 a-c Average annual employment growth in various sectors,
1980–1990 (per cent)

Source: OECD STAN database.

1980s. In all three areas, the sectors with the highest employment growth are mainly high-technology sectors, particularly in ICT. However, since 1990 the changes in defence procurement have strongly affected these sectors in the United States. Unfortunately, these statistics do not include software but, as already described in Chapter 3, this was a field of very high employment growth throughout the Triad.

4.4 Employment growth and productivity

On the basis of some recent OECD work (Sakurai, 1993) attempting to 'decompose' changes in employment, Figure 4.6 illustrates for the United States, Japan and the EU the 'decomposition' in employment growth between output growth (subdivided into domestic (final) demand and exports minus imports) and changes in technology (changes in input–output coefficients and labour productivity). While many questions can be raised about the assumed independence of each of those 'decomposed' factors, the figure illustrates quite neatly how the employment growth in the high-wage or high-tech industrial sectors observed in Figure 4.5 in the United States, Japan and to a lesser extent Europe was primarily the result of rapid output growth (both of domestic and foreign origin) which more than compensated for the very rapid growth in labour productivity in this sector. By contrast, the employment growth in financial and personal service sectors has gone hand in hand with minimal gains in labour productivity. Employment growth in these sectors has been primarily the result of rapid domestic output growth. Whether such employment growth is 'sustainable' or is simply the result of the failure of those sectors to use new ICT efficiently remains of course to be seen. Some studies of the financial sector forecast that efficiency improvements and the increased tradability of such services will reduce EC employment in financial services by more than 10 per cent in the 1990s and certainly many cases of 'down-sizing' in employment were reported by large banks in the early 1990s.

The variety of sources of employment growth in different sectors of the OECD countries considered in Figure 4.6 suggests that one has to be very careful in drawing general policy conclusions in the area of employment creation. Clearly, new demand and output growth associated with manufacturing can still be a provider of some employment growth. However, and as illustrated in the case of France, the

United Kingdom, the Netherlands, or even the United States, the growth in productivity, in order to stay competitive, might be so high that there is actually a decline in employment in some of these sectors. In services, old, traditional and above all 'non-tradable' demand for personal care services will generate many employment opportunities, given the low, sometimes negative, labour productivity in such sectors. At the same time though, new, increasingly tradable demand for finance and other business services, whose productivity growth pattern has varied in the United States, Japan and the EU, might cause major employment reductions in those sectors.

While the data reported in Figures 4.5 and 4.6 describe some of the structural changes in employment creation in the 1970s and 1980s, little evidence exists for the most recent period. However, there is little doubt that the intensity of structural change has accelerated in the recent recession, and that the variety in employment growth and decline patterns between countries and sectors has, if anything, increased. This means that the policies advanced to deal with unemployment must take full account of this diversity. We return to this point in Chapter 7.

a) United States

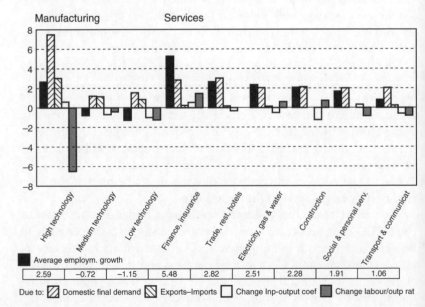

b) Japan

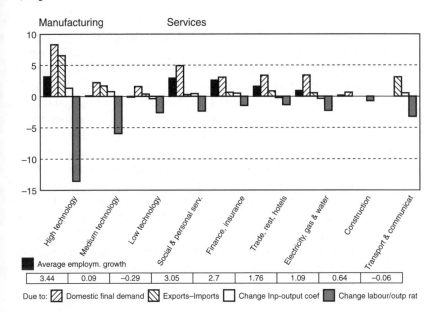

c) European Union

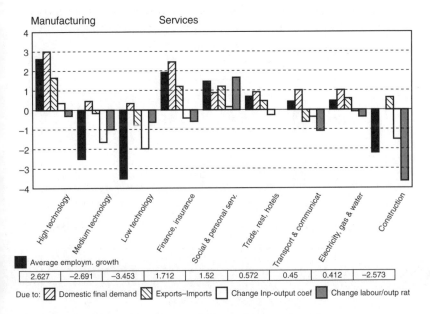

Figure 4.6 a-c Estimated growth in employment in various sectors, 1972–1985 (per cent p.a.)

Source: Sakurai (1993).

4.5 International trade and employment

As highlighted already in Figure 4.6, an important source of employment creation and also employment displacement is directly associated with foreign trade and international competitiveness. Based on
the OECD methodology used above, Figure 4.7 illustrates the
employment impact of trade for three categories of manufactured
commodities: high-, medium- and low-wage goods, for the United
States (Figure 4.7a), Japan (4.7b) and the EU (4.7c). The figure illustrates the crucial importance of foreign trade to employment growth
in Japan. More than 5.6 million jobs in manufacturing were created
in Japan over the period 1970–85 directly as a result of foreign trade.[1]
That is about three-quarters of the total gains in employment in
Japan over this period (Sakurai, 1993, p. 31). The 'full employment'
output growth pattern that Japan enjoyed over the 1970s and 1980s
was in other words primarily based on foreign output growth and
foreign market penetration. The employment gains were realised
both with respect to high, medium and even low wage sectors, and
with respect to trade with the OECD, so-called Dynamic Asian
Economies (DAE: Hong-Kong, Singapore, South Korea and Taiwan)
and China, and the Rest Of the World (ROW). While trade with the
OECD area remained over the period considered in Figure 4.7b
(1970–85) the most important employment growth contributing

a) United States

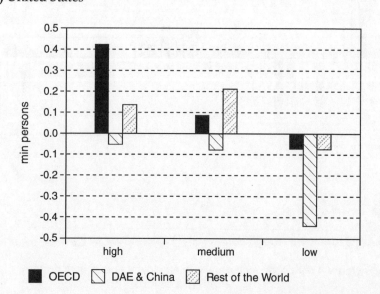

b) Japan

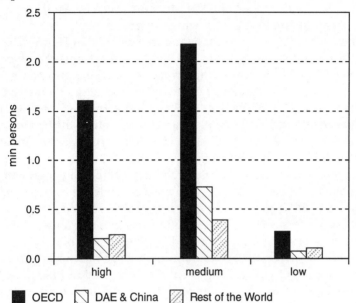

c) European Union

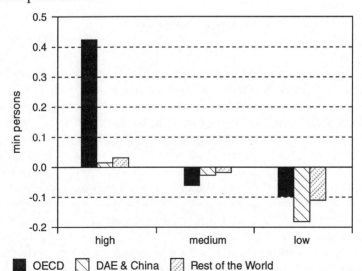

Figure 4.7 a-c Trade impacts on employment, 1972–1985
* DAE: Dynamic Asian Economics: Hong Kong, Singapore, South Korea
and Taiwan

Source: Sakurai, 1993.

factor in Japan, it is likely that over the more recent period trade with the DAE and the other SEA countries has become as, if not more, important for employment growth in Japan.

The United States by contrast, and as illustrated in Figure 4.7a, has barely relied on foreign markets for its output and employment growth. Only in the area of high wage commodities and non-manufacturing trade has employment growth been realised on the basis of foreign trade. Overall the United States lost about half a million jobs as a result of trade. These employment losses were in the first instance the result of trade with the DAEs and China, particularly in low wage commodities. Trade with the rest of the OECD particularly in high wage commodities still generated substantial employment growth.

Finally in the case of the EU (Figure 4.7c), while the overall employment gains and losses of trade appear to cancel each other more or less out, nearly all the employment gains in manufacturing appear to be the result of trade in high wage commodities with the rest of the OECD.

Given the importance of trade in high-wage/high-tech sectors for employment growth and the particular contribution therein of ICT commodities, we now turn to some more detailed data on the trade performance of the United States, Japan and the EU in ICT commodities.

4.6 International trade in ICT commodities

The great and growing importance of ICT goods in world trade is vividly illustrated in Tables 4.1 and 4.2. They are by far the fastest growing segment of world trade and Table 4.2 shows the astonishing success of East Asia. In Figure 4.8a, b and c, the trend in the absolute trade balance of the United States, Japan and the EU in ICT commodities over the 1980s is represented. The figure illustrates the dramatic trade surplus of Japan in ICT goods, which seems only to have come to stabilisation in 1987 at a staggering trade surplus level of about $67bn. It also illustrates the rapidly declining trade balance of the EC. Its trade deficit of $32bn is now more than twice the deficit of the United States in ICT goods.

Another less absolute and more comparative way to look at the trade performance of the ICT sectors is provided by indicators of international competitiveness such as the 'Revealed Comparative Advantage (RCA)' index which normalises the export performance of the ICT sector relative to the trade performance of all manufactured goods. Indices[2] above 0 indicate comparative advantage in the particular sector; indices below 0 comparative disadvantage.

Table 4.1 Rates of growth of exports, 1980–1989 (% annual increases)

All primary commodities	2
of which:	
Fuels	–5
Food	3
Raw materials	4
Ores, minerals	4
All manufactures	8
of which:	
Iron and steel	4
Textiles	6
Chemicals	7
Clothing	10
Machinery and transport	8
of which:	
ICT goods*	13

* Office machinery, telecom equipment and electronics.
Source: GATT (1990).

Table 4.2 Share of office machinery, telecom equipment and electronics in total merchandise exports (ranked by value of 1989 exports)

	1980	1989
1. Japan	14	28
2. USA	8	13
3. FRG	5	5
4. UK	5	9
5. Singapore	14	34
6. South Korea	10	22
7. Taiwan	14	25
8. Hong Kong	12	16
9. France	4	7
10. Netherlands	5	7

Source: GATT (1990), vol. II, p. 40, Table IV.

a) United States

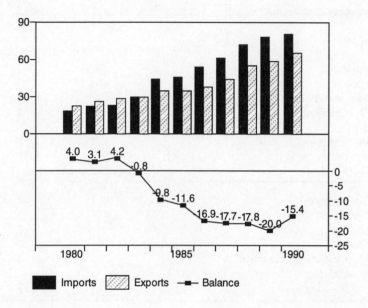

b) Japan

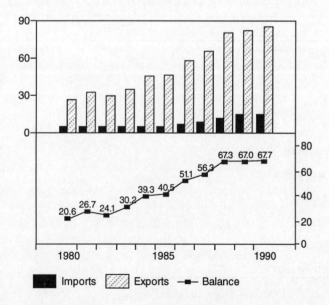

c) European Union

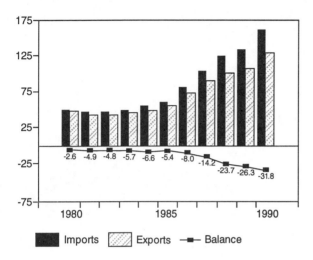

Figure 4.8 a-c Imports and exports of IT-sectors, 1980–1990 ($bn)

Source: OECD and MERIT Data Bases

We present in Figure 4.9 such normalised RCA indices for the United States, Japan and the various EU countries for the office equipment and computers sector (Figure 4.9a) and for the communications equipment sector (Figure 4.9b) over the last 20 years (three-year averages for the periods 1970–73 and 1988–90).

Figure 4.9a illustrates in the first instance the emergence of a significant comparative advantage of Japan in office equipment and computers over the last 20 years. In the case of the United States it points to a weakening but continuing comparative advantage in office equipment and computers. With respect to the EU, and possibly most strikingly, Figure 4.9a illustrates how Europe has further fallen behind and does not have a comparative advantage in office equipment and computers.

Finally, with respect to the individual EU countries, apart from the extraordinary but special case of Ireland with a dramatic, but primarily 'foreign assembly' comparative advantage in office equipment and computers, Figure 4.9a illustrates how each of the large European countries, with the exception of the United Kingdom, has lost its comparative advantage in this ICT sector. This is particularly the case for those EU countries with large domestic producers in office equipment and computers: Germany, France and Italy.

a) Office machines and computers

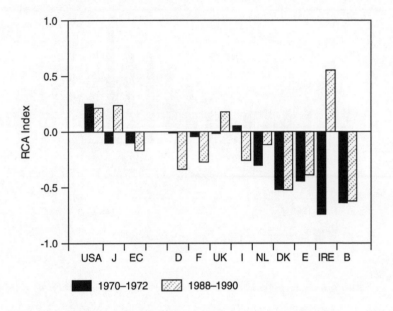

b) Communications equipment

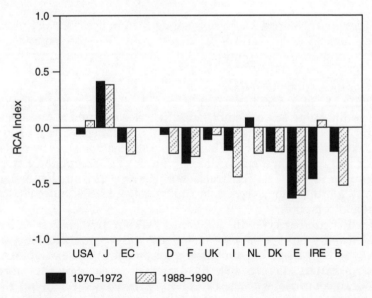

Figure 4.9 a-b Revealed comparative advantage index, 1970–1990

Source: MERIT.

In communications equipment (Figure 4.9b), the Japanese comparative advantage is dramatic. Only the United States and Ireland have today indices just above nil. Germany, the Netherlands and Italy, again all countries with large domestic firms in this ICT area, have seen their relative competitiveness decline significantly over the last 20 years.

In other words and as illustrated by both Figures 4.9a and 4.9b, except in the case of instruments, the areas where Europe seems to have increased and built up a comparative advantage in ICT appear to have been dominated by the activities of foreign, non-European firms. The large European countries with strong domestic firms appear all to have lost much of their competitive strength over the last 20 years in the two broad ICT sectors considered above.

The result has been, as Table 4.3 illustrates, a significant weakening of the EU 'Big 4' in comparative advantage for ICT goods. Yet, it is these goods which are top of the table in average annual growth performance.

Table 4.3 Commodity growth and comparative advantage

		Comparative advantage rank		
	Ave. annual growth 1979–87	Japan 1990/1965	USA 1990/1965	EU4* 1990/1965
1. Computers	20.4	7/33	11/6	53/17
2. Semiconductors	13.4	2/12	6/11	48/30
3. Telecom equipment	13.0	3/11	27/22	43/25
4. Consumer electronics	12.6	1/1	57/37	59/31
5. Instruments	12.3	26/22	19/7	14/27
6. Machinery for electricity	11.7	12/15	13/17	7/12
7. Clothing	11.1	48/6	56/39	16/7
8. Furniture	11.0	44/24	50/37	19/13
9. Road vehicles	10.8	6/19	43/20	45/2
10. Power gen. mach.	10.6	19/27	8/5	17/18

* France, Italy, Germany and the UK.

Note: In the comparative advantage (specialisation) ranking, the first number refers to the export specialisation of country in a particular product in 1990 and the second to the ranking in 1965. The basis for computing the ranking of comparative advantage is the total export of all OECD countries with the exception of Australia and New Zealand.

Source: Computations from OECD data.

The employment implications of this pattern are not easy to measure. The presence of many foreign firms in the ICT area in Europe has certainly generated much new employment which would otherwise not have been generated (see e.g. the evidence presented in Figure 4.6b). At the same time those firms have been much more active in reaping fairly early on the advantages of European integration. Compared with the United States, Japan or South East Asia, growth in Europe in ICT has lagged behind and Europe's world market share has steadily declined.

The shift in comparative advantage away from high-tech commodities, towards more traditional commodities, as highlighted in Table 4.3, has, in our view, had a major negative impact on European growth and employment. The results are: a much slower pattern of diffusion of ICT equipment to the rest of the economy; a much lower birth rate of new product or service activities in the ICT area; much higher prices for telecommunication services and ICT commodities; and a far less dynamic and competitive ICT industry.

4.7 Growth in service employment, service tradability and ICT

In Chapter 3 we already referred to the overall pervasiveness of information and communication technology. The pervasive influence of ICT on services is particularly worthwhile emphasising from an international perspective. With respect to services, ICT appears to have a specific trade-'enlarging' impact, which in our view is rather different from manufacturing. Services can be defined here, following Quinn (1986), as those activities (sectors) where output is essentially consumed when produced. One could think of going to an opera or theatre and listening to a live performance or having a haircut. The traditional more pragmatic definition of services, i.e. everything other than agriculture, extraction, manufacturing, construction and utilities, is of course a much broader but less coherent definition. The lack of analytical coherence of this 'service' definition might also explain why economists have generally tended to ignore the study and analysis of service activities. The traditionally suggested classification of services is generally a functional one (Browning and Singelmann, 1978; Guy, 1987). There are distributive services, such as wholesale and retail trade, producer services including intermediate services, personal and other social services. It is obvious that ICT will have trade-enlarging impacts in each of those service sectors, but is also clear that those impacts will be very different from sector to sector, particularly within the possibly *international* trade-enlarging impact of ICT on services. The distinction between 'sheltered' and 'open' service sectors or service activities is a crucial one for any present discussion on future employment growth, as we will see in Chapter 7. Before doing so, however, it is essential to analyse how ICT has continuously opened up or increased the tradability of traditionally sheltered or relatively closed service activities.

Information technology, almost by definition, will allow for the increased tradability of service activities, particularly those which have been most constrained by the geographical or time proximity of production and consumption. By bringing in a space or *time/storage* dimension, information technology will make possible the separation of production from consumption in an increasing number of such activities. This was certainly the case with regard to the invention of printing in the Middle Ages and the impact this first new information technology had on the limited tradable 'service' activity of monks copying manuscripts by hand. It was the time/storage dimension of the new printing technology which opened up access to information in the most dramatic and pervasive way and led, to use Marx's words, to the 'renaissance of science', the growth of universities, education, libraries, the spreading of culture, etc. This opening-up, 'tradability' effect would become of far more importance to the future growth and development of Western society than the emergence of a new, in this case purely manufacture-based, printing industry.

In the case of the current 'new' information technologies and their potential to collect, store, process and diffuse enormous quantities of information at minimal costs, both the time/storage and space dimensions of the new technology can be expected to bring about the further opening-up of many service activities, increasing their domestic *and* international tradability. As in the case of the telephone, it is likely that the 'new' information technologies manufacturing sector (in the first instance the computer manufacturing sector) will remain relatively small compared to the growth and size of the information technologies service-producing sector. It will be the indirect 'trade' effects resulting from the use of information technologies in many services which will be most important, both in terms of employment and of output growth.

As a parenthesis and following on from the analysis presented in Chapter 3, the impact of information and communication technologies in manufacturing could well be characterised as exactly of an opposite nature. Rather than bringing time/storage or space between production and consumption as in services, information technology in its manufacturing user impact will in the first instance aim at *reducing* the time/storage or space dimension between production and consumption. Many of the most distinctive characteristics of the new information technologies discussed in Chapter 3 are related directly to the potential of the new technology to link up networks of component and material suppliers, thus allowing for reductions in storage and production time costs — typified in the so-called Just-in-Time production system. At the same time, the increased flexibility associated with the new technology allows for a closer integration of production with demand, thus reducing the firm's own storage and inventory costs — which could be typified as Just-in-Time selling (e.g. Benetton). Both features seem to work in the opposite direction from what was said above with regard to services, i.e. they aim at reducing the time/storage dimension between production and consumption. In doing so they will also reduce the 'tradability' of a number of those intermediary storage and inventory manufacturing activities.

The increased potential for flexibility and decentralisation associated with the new information technologies can also be expected to reduce the geographical *space* dimension between production and consumption in many manufacturing sectors. The relative increase in physical (production or person) as opposed to information transport costs might well lead e.g. to closer location of production units to consumer markets, particularly once the environnmental costs of transport are taken into account. We discuss this issue in more detail in Chapter 6.

4.8 International relocation: from manufacturing to services?

Not surprisingly, one of the most sensitive and newly emerging issues in the technology employment debate is the role played by ICT in the increased international tradability of services and international relocation of manufacturing, and increasingly also service activities. As we discussed above, the underlying concern is here one of a new international re- or delocation pattern resulting directly from the rapidly growing possibilities associated with the use of ICT.

With respect to manufacturing there is now growing evidence of the significant negative impact on the demand for unskilled labour in manufacturing in developed countries because of increased trade competition in such activities from industrialising 'Southern' countries.

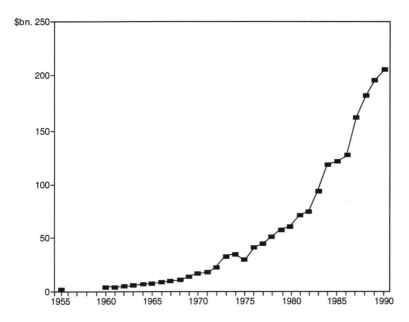

Figure 4.10 Manufactured exports of the South to the North
(billions of constant 1980 dollars)

Note: Data in current dollars for 1955 and 1960–88 from UNCTAD (1976, 1983, 1982–90).
Source: Wood (1994).

Evidence originally gathered by Wood (1994, p.12), and presented in Figure 4.10, illustrates the dramatic nature of the increase in Southern exports of manufactures to the North in the 1980s.

This rapid growth in manufacturing exports from the South has gone hand in hand with a growing gap in manufacturing wages between OECD countries and the South and a narrowing gap between productivity levels. In Figure 4.11 we illustrate this trend using a relative unit labour cost indicator which we have called *delocalisation pressure*. It is based on the gap in labour costs between the low-wage and high-wage country, corrected for the gap in labour productivity between the two countries. The indicator illustrates how over the last ten years the delocalisation pressure has increased significantly between Europe (and in particular Germany) and the South and East Asian economies. For the United States and Japan the rise in delocalisation pressure has been less pronounced.

Not surprisingly, there is growing concern with a much more general trend towards delocalisation involving practically all manufac-

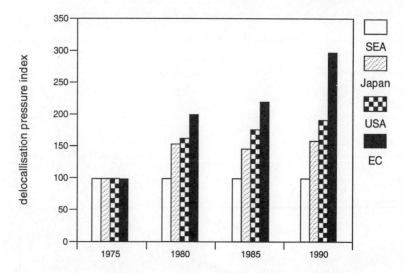

Figure 4.11 Delocalisation pressure= labour cost (constant prices, per man-hour) divided by labour productivity (= output per manhour) (1975=100)

Source: MERIT, ILO, OECD

turing sectors and an increasing number of service sectors. Such, more generic international relocation, often associated with global, footloose, multinational corporations 'delocalising' production activity towards regions/countries with lower labour costs, will undoubtedly be a major and continuing source of employment decline in manufacturing in high-wage developed OECD countries. This relocalisation concern is not just expressed with respect to delocalisation to the industrialising South, typified in Figure 4.11 by South and East Asia, but also more and more within Europe, because of the geographical proximity of new, low labour cost regions in the ex-socialist, East European countries, and because of the lack of agreement over a 'social charter' in the Maastricht Treaty of European Union which might prevent convergence in the social sphere, at least in the short run. An extreme but exceptional example because of both geographical and cultural factors has been the large number of Finnish firms locating part of their activities in Estonia in the early 1990s.

Such trends towards generic delocalisation are to some extent within the logic of international competition, the growing emergence of the global company and the deregulation of international capital flows. However, while national governments might be unable to do much about such delocalisation trends, local government authorities have, in our view, a much more active role to play in 'keeping' such firms within their region. Indeed, local government authorities have a prime responsibility in creating economic conditions to ensure that subsidiaries of foreign firms become embedded in the domestic economy, so that the region in which they are located becomes essential to the subsidiary's competitiveness. From this perspective, local authorities might well have to focus less on attracting foreign firms with subsidies, and switch their attention more to creating favourable infrastructural conditions that will strongly link foreign subsidiaries to the local region. These infrastructural conditions include education and training, networking with small and medium-sized local subcontracting firms, and collaboration with local universities and technical institutes or other research organisations. We shall return to some of these policy issues in Chapter 7, but it will be clear that such policies will aim at reducing the locational flexibility of both multi-national and national corporations by strengthening the attractiveness of the existing location.

A new and additional important factor in the discussion of delocalisation is of course the particular role ICT might play with respect to future relocalisation of newly made tradable service activities. This brings us to the particular and, from an employment perspective, crucial role of non-tradables as an absorbing sector of low-skilled, low-wage employment particularly in developed high-wage economies. It has often been claimed that the non-tradable service sector in Japan acted as an employment 'reservoir' in times of slack demand, both within the large firms, organised along lifelong employment, and in the economy at large with many relatively low-skilled service activities. The steady low levels of unemployment in Japan are thus also explained by the cushioning effect of the non-tradable sector. There are, however, good arguments that the non tradable service sector has been shrinking significantly over the last ten years in all OECD countries, and in the EU in particular.

First and foremost, as discussed above, ICT has significantly increased the tradability and geographical mobility of many service activities. The present trend in many service sectors towards the relocation of service activities such as programming, simple clerical functions, and reservations and bookings illustrates the fact that information and communication technology has brought about a rapid and cheap flow of information across the world, creating to some extent the global service village. As one software executive put it, competitors are no longer ten thousand miles away, they are one micro-second away. Labour cost differences in such service activities are the major cost variable. Firms, even those which had little international experience, are '(re)discovering' the basic principles of the international division of labour.

But there might well be a much more fundamental trend underlying such international relocation shifts in services. Many Western firms are also discovering the relatively high levels of human capital in many Asian countries. The latter, after years of heavy investment in education, particularly in the science, technical and engineering fields, are starting to reap some of the benefits of these investments and attract some of the complementary physical capital. Whether this is a reflection of a more lateral division of labour or whether this is the result of a much more straightforward process of catching up is an open question. What is certain, though, is that an increasing number of jobs in OECD countries, even in high-skilled activities, that were previously protected because they were essentially non-tradable, are becoming subject to international competition. It is this new pressure across the occupational spectrum and across the manufacturing services divide which probably gives rise to some of the most outspoken fears of low-wage competition and rapid growth in structural unemployment in the OECD economies.

Notes

[1] It should be emphasised that the 'decomposition' methodology used by Sakurai (1993) and illustrated in Figure 4.7 only allows for directly attributable employment gains/losses due to foreign trade. Indirect effects, e.g. through increased competition, are not taken into account.

[2] The RCA index has been normalised as $(RCA-1)/(RCA+1)$.

5

'A MAN'S PLACE IS IN THE HOME': various
forms of flexibility

5.1 Introduction

Almost everyone now agrees that *flexibility* is essential to overcome structural unemployment but this means very different things to different people. Traditionally, classical and neo-classical economic theory placed the main emphasis on *wage* flexibility and on the *mobility* of labour. According to many economic historians (e.g. Dobb, 1946), the breakdown of serfdom and other feudal limitations on the movement of labour was essential to the growth of a capitalist labour market. The so-called 'second serfdom' or preservation of feudal institutions in Eastern Europe is often advanced as the main explanation for the delay in the spread of industrialisation from Western Europe. Historians have also placed great emphasis on international migration as well as the migration of workers from country to towns. In Third World countries where a high proportion of the labour force is still employed in agriculture this migration is still the main source of flexibility in the supply of unskilled workers. The growth of an industrial proletariat obliged to sell their labour power was an absolutely necessary condition for the rise of capitalist industry.

Now that the share of agricultural employment in most OECD countries has fallen to a very low level this source has dwindled. The increasing attempts to limit or stop the flows of international migration (except within the European Union)[1] have had two major consequences. On the one hand, as we have seen in Chapter 4, there has been a change in the international division of labour with increasingly strong competition from low-wage countries where the supply of unskilled labour is still extremely flexible in the traditional sense. From this perspective the evidence presented by Wood (1994) and reported in Figure 4.10 is illustrative of the new emerging low-wage employment pressure on unskilled labour in the Northern developed countries. The pressure from the South for international downward wage equalisation of the North's unskilled labour, whether through international migration or imports of goods and services, is undoubtedly a new and crucial flexibility pressure. On the other hand, since the Second World War the 'participation rate' of women in the labour force has steadily grown in the industrialised countries (Table 5.1). Of course, there are many other factors which have led to this rise in women's participation, such as the fall in family size and the change in women's attitudes, together with legislative changes, but the demand from employers usually for lower-cost labour has also been essential.

However, this basic type of flexibility affecting mainly the supply of unskilled workers and their wage rates is only one type of flexibility. Other equally important types of flexibility are the ways in which work is organised and the ways in which the work-force acquire new skills. Without adequate training and education no amount of unskilled labour could develop or produce many of the complex products and services of modern industrial economies. Even well-trained and educated workers could not cope with the speed of change in product mix and process technology without flexible organisations and contracting arrangements between firms and individuals. As we have seen in Chapter 3, one of the main characteristics of the ICT techno-economic paradigm is flexibility in design, manufacturing, marketing and delivery of services. Moreover, as we shall argue in Chapter 6, ICT has the potential to reduce the need for geographical mobility. Whereas during the industrial revolution increased flexibility was achieved by switching labour from domestic 'cottage' industries to factory production systems, the reverse can often be the case now and there are strong environmental protection grounds for using and reinforcing this potential.

To achieve these other types of organisational and skill flexibility is far more difficult than to achieve traditional labour supply flexibility; the change in skill composition which is needed for the ICT paradigm is probably greater than for any other technological revolution. However, the alternative to competing in high-skill, high value-added types of manufacturing and service activities is to compete in low-skill or unskilled labour with countries which have far lower wage

Table 5.1 Labour force participation rates by sex, 1973–1992 (%)

	Men						Women					
	1973	1979	1983	1990	1991	1992[c]	1973	1979	1983	1990	1991	1992[c]
Australia	91.1	87.6	85.9	85.9	85.6	85.3	47.7	50.3	52.1	62.1	62.2	62.4
Austria	83.0	81.6	82.2	80.1	80.5	81.3	48.5	49.1	49.7	55.4	56.3	58.3
Belgium	83.2	79.3	76.8	72.7	72.8	—	41.3	46.3	48.7	52.4	53.2	—
Canada	86.1	86.3	84.7	84.9	83.9	83.4	47.2	55.5	60.0	68.1	68.1	67.9
Denmark	89.6	89.6	87.6	89.6	88.5	—	61.9	69.9	74.2	78.4	78.9	—
Finland	80.0	82.2	82.0	80.6	79.6	78.5	63.6	68.9	72.7	72.9	71.8	70.6
France	85.2	82.6	78.4	74.6	74.5	—	50.1	54.2	54.4	56.1	56.8	—
Germany	89.6	84.9	82.6	80.8	80.6	80.1	50.3	52.2	52.5	57.0	58.1	59.0
Greece	83.2	79.0	80.0	82.1	—	—	32.1	32.8	40.4	39.9	—	—
Ireland	92.3	88.7	87.1	82.2	81.9	—	34.1	35.2	37.8	38.9	39.9	—
Italy	85.1	82.6	80.7	78.9	79.4	79.2	33.7	38.7	40.3	44.9	45.8	46.3
Japan	90.1	89.2	89.1	87.8	88.9	89.3	54.0	54.7	57.2	60.4	61.5	61.7
Luxembourg	93.1	88.9	85.1	—	77.7	—	35.9	39.8	41.7	—	44.8	—
Netherlands	85.6	79.0	77.3	79.9	80.3	—	29.2	33.4	40.3	53.0	54.5	—
New Zealand	89.2	87.3	84.7	82.2	82.3	83.0	39.2	45.0	45.7	62.4	62.8	—
Norway	86.5	89.2	87.2	84.5	82.9	—	50.6	61.7	65.5	71.2	71.1	70.9
Portugal[a]	100.8	90.9	87.6	86.1	85.9	—	32.1	57.3	57.2	60.4	62.8	—
Spain	92.9	83.1	80.2	76.8	76.0	74.9	33.4	32.6	33.2	40.9	41.2	42.1
Sweden	88.1	87.9	85.9	85.3	84.5	82.7	62.6	72.8	76.6	81.1	80.3	78.7
Switzerland[b]	100.6	94.6	93.5	96.2	95.3	—	54.1	53.0	55.2	59.6	59.8	—
United Kingdom	93.0	90.5	87.5	86.5	86.1	85.6	53.2	58.0	57.2	65.3	64.5	64.5
United States	86.2	85.7	84.6	85.8	84.7	85.0	51.1	58.9	61.8	68.6	68.4	68.9
North America	86.2	85.8	84.6	85.7	84.6	84.8	50.7	58.6	61.6	68.5	68.4	68.8
OECD Europe[d]	88.7	84.8	82.3	80.6	78.3	—	44.7	48.6	49.8	54.8	54.0	—
Total OECD[d]	88.2	85.9	84.3	83.7	82.4	—	48.3	53.1	55.1	60.7	60.5	—

[a] Labour force data include a significant number of persons aged less than 15 years.
[b] Data disaggregated by age and sex exclude a certain number of foreign seasonal workers; these are included in the estimates of the working population.
[c] Secretariat estimates.
[d] Above countries only.

Source: OECD (1993), Employment Outlook, p. 192.

rates and longer hours of work. The dilemma confronting the OECD countries is that they are faced simultaneously with pressures for both types of flexibility — the old type based on an unskilled proletariat obliged to accept lower wages from time to time and the new type based on new skills, new management systems and new types of work organisation and industrial relations. As Tony Jackson (1994) put it pithily in *The Financial Times* of 25 February: 'Either get smarter or else get poorer.'

The recent Interim Report by the OECD Secretary-General (OECD, June 1993) especially highlights this dilemma for *European* countries:

Wage structures in some countries have moved out of line with the structure of employment opportunities: employers are unable to offer some
types of job and remain profitable ... Those most likely to be hit by technological change, shifts in trade and dislocations of production are the
least skilled, or those whose skills are too narrow. The natural tendency,
in the absence of any countervailing policy, social force, or institution, is
for wage differentials to reflect the decreasing demand for unskilled
labour and the increasing demand for skilled labour. Such a development
— as has happened in the United States — slows the process of job loss
for unskilled workers. But this is achieved at the risk of creating a larger
class of the 'working poor' and, at the limit, of significant withdrawal
from the labour force. (p. 29)

As we have seen in Chapter 4, whereas in the 1970s most economists specialising in international trade would have argued that job losses directly due to imports from low-wage countries were relatively insignificant, Adrian Wood (1994) has presented a powerful argument that they had become very important by the 1990s (Figure 4.10 in Chapter 4). There are many reasons for this change; among the most important are the liberalisation of capital markets and the far greater flexibility of firms in locating their investments and their sources of supply. In other words the flexibility and mobility of *capital* increased much more than that of labour.

The OECD Report argues that the setting of minimum wage levels may tend to make the unskilled unemployed and that the policy of compressing wage differentials has been undermined by technical change and international competition. It therefore suggests that the 'low skilled jobs have to be low paid but training policies should pre-vent people from becoming trapped in them'. Low-wage jobs, according to this view, are valuable in giving work experience, espe-cially to young workers and to immigrant workers, but on a purely temporary, not a long-term basis. To some extent the Delors White Paper (CEC, 1993) also accepts this view.

Clearly the *time* dimension is the critical element here in considering the strategies proposed by the OECD. Whether the outcome is ultimately a permanent underclass (as envisaged by some of the 'segmentation' analysis in the United States) or a more skilled, better-paid and fully employed work-force depends on the varying national capabilities to promote rapid technical and institutional change and to upgrade skills quickly. These are the subject of the final chapter. In this chapter we first discuss wage flexibility and the role of unemployment in sustaining wage flexibility and mobility. Then we discuss organisational flexibility and working time arrangements, and finally the problems of flexibility in skills.

5.2 Wage flexibility

As we have seen in Chapter 2, the classical and neo-classical theories of employment and technical change rely on various compensation mechanisms to bring about the necessary adjustments to clear the labour market, i.e. to balance the supply and demand for labour. Central to these processes of adjustment are flexibility in the prices of labour and capital, i.e. the wage rate and the rate of interest. However, it was usually recognised that although the price of labour might be described as a 'price' like any other, and labour might be conceived as a commodity like any other, in fact the labour market had some very specific features, which meant that it was actually never strictly comparable to these other markets. From the earliest days of the Industrial Revolution, workers sought to combine in trade unions to improve their conditions of employment and those of their children. Reciprocally, employers and governments which they supported attempted sometimes to make such combinations illegal (as in the British Combination Acts of 1799 or later anti-union legislation in other countries) or to restrict the powers of unions in various ways. Not surprisingly, resistance to the *downward* movement of wages was always an exceptionally acute social problem even in the absence of trade-union organisation, whilst *upward* movements in times of labour shortages or great trade-union strength (or both) could sometimes contribute to inflationary pressures. These and other special features of the labour market meant that 'labour economics' and 'industrial relations' became specialised branches of economics in which social and institutional factors were always prominent.

One of the outstanding post-war labour economists, Henry Phelps-Brown (1975), suggested in a highly original short paper a long-wave theory of industrial relations which neatly complements the long-wave theories of Kondratieff and Schumpeter described in Chapter 2. Phelps-Brown made an analogy between the period of industrial militancy in the years preceding the First World War and the European 'pay explosion' and strike wave of the 1960s and 1970s. Both periods were characterised by intense shop-floor militancy on the part of younger workers, sometimes in defiance of older-established union officials and the 'normal' procedures. The Phelps-Brown paper was written before the drastic changes in labour legislation introduced by the Thatcher government in Britain in the 1980s and similar trends in the United States and elsewhere. Nevertheless, these events have only served to confirm the validity of his analogy. The 1920s and 1930s (the 'downturn' of the Third Kondratieff Long Wave) were characterised by prolonged attempts to weaken unions and to achieve downward flexibility in wages. This led to the General Strike in Britain in 1926, followed by the reduction in miners' wages, and in many other countries, such as Germany, to the outright prohibition of unions.

The periods of high growth and relatively full employment during the *belle époque* before the First World War and again in the 1950s and 1960s ultimately generated inflationary wage cost pressures which proved increasingly difficult to contain. Only after a fairly prolonged period did these pressures recede. Phelps-Brown stresses the long period of time which it takes for the attitudes and expectations of both workers and employers to adjust to changed circumstances. Workers and unions who had experienced the Great Depression of the 1930s were very cautious about pressing wage claims in the 1950s even though their bargaining position was then far stronger because of full employment. But a new young generation of workers no longer felt constrained by the inhibitions of their elders, so that rank and file grass-roots militancy became widespread in the pay explosion and strike wave of the late 1960s.

An Italian economist, Michele Salvati (1984) has drawn attention to the parallels between the Phelps-Brown paper and the much earlier brilliant forecast of Kalecki (1943) on the political consequences of full employment. Kalecki realised that Keynesian economics would dramatically change the post-war management of the economies of industrialised countries.[2] On the one hand, this would generate 'electoral business cycles' as governments strove to enhance their popularity (whether successfully or not) by pre-electoral Keynesian manipulation. This did indeed become a familiar feature of the post-war political and economic scene just as Kalecki had foreseen. However, Kalecki also drew attention to a more fundamental problem. The repeated manipulation of the economy by Keynesian techniques for political purposes (in a way which Keynes himself would not have condoned) could lead to acute social conflicts. Labour discipline, he pointed out, depended in a capitalist system of indus-trial relations, at the last resort on the sack. Full employment could lead to a breakdown in labour discipline and would therefore be increasingly uncomfortable for employers, their joint organisations and the political parties which they supported and sponsored. By combining the ideas of Kalecki with those of Phelps-Brown, Salvati proposed an illuminating theory of long waves in labour relations and inflationary cost pressures which complements the approach of Schumpeter to waves of new investment.

In fact, most economists have come to accept both the over-whelming importance of institutional factors in industrial relations and the long time-lags in the adjustment of inflationary expectations and bargaining behaviour. Two of the main innovations in the post-war theory of employment and inflation could both be regarded as attempts to grapple with these changing long-term relationships — the 'Phillips Curve' and the so-called 'NAIRU' (non-accelerating inflation rate of unemployment). Neither of these is uncontroversial (see e.g., Worswick, 1991, Ormerod, 1994), but those who expect the rate to be more stable have missed the main point, which is precisely that the rate of unemployment which supposedly might mitigate or aggravate inflationary behaviour does indeed change over time and varies between countries, depending on institutional factors.

As the OECD (1993) pointed out, nearly half of the EU unemployed had been out of work for more than a year in 1992. The effects could be clearly seen, for example, in the recent work of Layard who has been one of the most prolific and original researchers on unemploy-ment over the past 20 years or so. Whereas, in his earlier work he was concerned mainly with the relationship between unemployment, incomes policy and inflation (the so-called NAIRU figured strongly in this argumentation — see Layard and Nickell, 1985), in his more recent work the emphasis shifted much more to active labour market policies to deal with *long-term* unemployment. In part, of course, this change of emphasis reflects simply the growth and persistence of long-term unemployment, especially in Europe, but it also reflects the diminution of inflationary pressures, which were much more acute in the 1970s and 1980s. In fact, one conclusion of two labour economists

(Blanchard and Diamond, 1988) was that a reduction in unemployment in Europe was now no longer likely to aggravate inflationary problems. Patrick Minford, a leading monetarist economist, has argued that the NAIRU fell from 11 per cent in the 1980s to 3 per cent in 1993. Whereas the earlier debate concentrated on the downward *inflexibility* of wages in Europe (e.g. Hayek, 1980) as a major explanation of the strong contrast between rates of job creation in the United States and Europe, Layard and Philpott dismissed this point abruptly in 1991:

the harshness of the US labour market has its casualties. Wages are far more unequal than in Europe, and have become much more so in the 1980s — with massive falls in living standards for the poorest workers. Low investment in skills has contributed to this ... Our view is clear. We should not follow the US model. We do not want a US-style underclass. (p. 7)

Instead of the US reliance on market forces and wage flexibility, Layard and Philpott rely heavily on active labour market policies in the British case through an amalgamation of local employment services with training and enterprise councils. However, like many US economists, they also lay great stress on the dangers of a 'culture of dependence' developing over time as a result of long-term unemployment and on the results of recent research which shows that employers are reluctant to hire workers who have been unemployed for 12 months or more. To break these 'vicious circle' phenomena requires in their view a whole series of inter connected active measures with a strong emphasis on training and an obligation to accept work or training combined with financial pressures and inducements, both for employers and for the unemployed. The emphasis on training and institutional change is characteristic of many European studies and demonstrates the shift away from wage-flexibility arguments towards emphasis on other types of flexibility. The so-called 'Jobs Summit' in Detroit in March 1994 indicated that some leading US economists advising the Clinton administration share this approach.

Their view is of course by no means uncontested. There are certainly many labour market economists both in North America and in Europe who would still put the main emphasis on the need to reduce relative wages (and social benefits) for less skilled workers and for young workers. In this more traditional vision much of the blame for the rise in unemployment, particularly in Europe, is still put on the lack of downward wage flexibility to enlarge the employment creation potential at the low-skill/low-wage end. In this view, the combination of existing income tax structures[3] and minimum wage legislation discourages the supply of low-paid work, and the amount of unemployment and social assistance benefits might have removed incentives for unemployed workers to seek more actively for work.

As the long-wave context demonstrates, the wage-flexibility argument cannot be discussed purely in static economic terms. Moreover, as we already argued in Chapter 1, the issue is not just an economic one. How to compensate for the fact that downward wage adjustment puts most of the burden of the adjustment on the economically weakest groups in society? How to avoid that the employment generated leads to 'work in poverty'? Minimum wages and many other social achievements at the low end of the labour market have been created because they corresponded, often in an absolute sense, to minimum renumeration levels, where life in work meant life with an income which would allow somebody to survive, given relative costs of living. Over time, these minimum wage levels could well have exceeded such 'survival' levels in some OECD countries, such as the Netherlands, but minimum wages, if calculated in 'purchasing power parities', are generally not high enough to offer much room for downward adjustment in many European countries without generating work in poverty.

Second, the question can be raised to what extent such immediate wage adjustments would not have severe, long-term negative consequences for both labour productivity growth and competitiveness. Whereas from a static, short-term point of view such policies might well generate low-skill employment possibilities in the non-tradable service sector — the so-called 'hamburger economy' or 'shoe-shine boy economy' — and thus reduce some of the structural long-term, low-skill unemployment, there exists a real danger that these measures could also lead to downward pressure on labour productivity with spill-overs to the tradable sectors, such as sweat shops in clothing and textiles, and a move towards long-term specialisation in low-skill activities. The preliminary indications of the effects of the abolition of wage councils in the United Kingdom are that they have indeed led to wage reductions in the relevant industries. But as Winston Churchill himself argued, this results in bad employers driving out more responsible ones, but not necessarily in an increase of employment. As we analysed in Chapter 4, it is precisely the low-wage sector which has, because of increased import penetration, suffered most employment losses.

Paradoxically, the wage-flexibility argument appears, from this perspective, rather similar to the argument for full protectionism. If there were full protectionism, for instance, at the broad level of the EU trade bloc (or even the new European economic space), low-skill employment would be likely to be generated in many of the labour-intensive, low-wage sectors which would now substitute for previous imports of such commodities. The new employment created would be substantially higher than the employment decline in the EU's world export sectors and full employment would probably be quickly rein-stalled. Apart from the obvious welfare losses from EU autarchy, the loss of the dynamic competitive impact of foreign imports would, however, in the long term, severely undermine the EU's growth and competitiveness. In an open world, downward wage adjustment appears to be the same type of escape from adjustment as protec-tionism. Introducing it as a main policy device could, from this per-spective, lead to the 'import of underdevelopment': a process of a more *lateral international division of labour*, where wage differentials within the developed countries increasingly resemble wage differen-tials between countries.

5.3 Organisational flexibility

So far in this chapter we have argued that in a long-term historical perspective the dangers of inflation have diminished greatly com-pared with the 1970s or 1980s and that the arguments for downward pressures on wages, which may have had some validity then, are no longer of such great importance. This does not mean that wage–cost inflation will never return. On the contrary, the long-wave perspec-tive suggests that it probably will but perhaps not in an acute form for another two decades, towards the peak of the next long-wave boom. It is not too early to think about such long-term problems and in the final policy chapter we make some suggestions about how they might be addressed. Institutional changes are in our view essential to give the necessary long-term confidence and stability in industrial rela-tions.

The fact that inflationary pressures have substantially diminished does not mean of course that wage flexibility is no longer an issue at all in a return to higher levels of employment. International competi-tive pressures are likely to intensify still further for the reasons advanced in Chapter 4, and even in non-tradable sectors of the economy the classical economic argument may still have some validity. However, from a social, economic and technological point of view the alternative path of a rapid shift to high-skill, high value-added activities is greatly to be preferred to the low-wage solution.

In the early decades of the nineteenth century it was the British industrialist Robert Owen who, in his factory at New Lanark, in his writings and his political activity, most clearly provided an alternative to the prevalent pessimistic Malthusian trend in classical economics at that time. Most industrialists and economists in the early days of the industrial revolution tended to assume that population pressures and the necessity to sustain profitability would persistently drive wages down to or below subsistence level. Particularly in times of recession most industrialists and their political spokesmen insisted that social reforms, such as shorter working hours or restrictions on the employ-ment of children would lead to the ruin of industry because they would reduce profitability and competitiveness.

Owen maintained that better work organisation, better education and training (he had his own school at New Lanark), social reforms and superior technology would together make it possible to offset such downward pressures and indeed to raise profitability. Later, Marx also recognised that the tendency to a falling rate of profit which he had identified could be offset by technical and organisa-tional innovations and by the opening of new markets. Schumpeter followed him in his model of the profits of innovative entrepreneurs, diffused through imitation and band-wagon effects and then gradu-ally eroded until a further set of innovations once more temporarily counteracted the tendency to diminishing returns.

There have thus been two main coexisting approaches to the restoration of profitability during cyclical downturns. The immediate response of many industrialists and bankers and the policy-makers whom they advise is to cut labour costs by reducing the labour force and ultimately by reducing wages. The latter is of course far from easy because of resistance from the work-force. For this reason poli-cies designed to weaken the bargaining power of trade unions are characteristic of long-wave downturns and have been particularly evident in the 1980s, as in the 1930s, the 1880s and the 1820s. Since the prevalence of mass unemployment may be insufficient, legislation to weaken trade unions or even outright prohibition of unions have often been features of these downturns. The actions of the UK gov-ernment were very much in line with this traditional approach: a suc-cession of laws on industrial relations in the 1980s culminating in a policy for reduction of real wages in the public sector in 1992–3 and the abolition of the wages councils — organisations set up by

Churchill in 1909 specifically to protect the lowest paid workers. One difficulty with these policies is that in a severe recession they may weaken aggregate consumer demand and thus aggravate the downturn by perpetuating Keynesian unemployment.

Galbraith (1992) has put forward an argument in his *Culture of Contentment* that social pressures to slip into a long-term high-unemployment equilibrium may be even stronger in the 1990s than in the 1930s. A coalition of the social groups who do quite well out of high interest rates, low growth and high unemployment in his view underlies recent social and political trends. If there is some validity in Galbraith's analysis (and we believe there is), then this makes it all the more urgent to address other types of flexibility going beyond the traditional theory of wage flexibility. Therefore in this section we address the question of organisational flexibility and working arrangements and in the following section we address the question of skills. As in Owen's day, employers and political organisations are divided in the relative emphasis which they place on different types of flexibility. Whilst we would accept that there is substance in all the various approaches, we believe that the main danger now lies in underestimating the role of these other types of flexibility.

In Chapter 3 we indicated in our description of the development of the ICT techno-economic paradigm that amongst its leading characteristics is greatly increased flexibility in product mix, process change, design, manufacturing systems (FMS, etc.), marketing response to changes in consumer demand, and in delivery of services including ultimately tele-shopping, tele-banking, tele-conferencing and tele-working, all now rapidly developing. This enhanced flexibility cannot be achieved without flexibility within the firm and between firms in their subcontracting relationships and alliances. One of the main reasons for the collapse of the militarised centrally planned economics of Eastern Europe was their inflexibility in all these dimensions. They actually coped quite well, relatively speaking, with the growth of heavy industry based (quite explicitly) on Fordist and Taylorist ideas of management and work organisation. Economic growth in Eastern Europe in the 1950s and early 1960s was relatively strong and they were 'catching up'. But they completely lacked the flexibility to adapt to the very different needs of ICT.

Nor is this transition easy for the more flexible capitalist market economies. They too suffer from innumerable institutional rigidities in their management systems, working practices, standards, regulation systems and so forth. An important source of flexibility in market economies has always lain in subcontracting, enabling firms to adjust to the changes in the pattern and timing of their new orders, which can rarely be precisely predicted. Small firms and self-employed individuals play an exceptionally important role in achieving this type of flexibility which is one reason why the centrally planned economies found it so difficult to achieve (even though they had their own semi-legal intermediaries in the system). The rapid establishment and growth of new small firms (SMEs) has been recognised everywhere as essential to renewal of employment growth and flexibility. Fluctuating and changing workloads, however, require not only flexibility in changing consortia and partnerships, but also flexibility in working time. The traditional 40- or 48-hour working week, with two to four weeks annual holiday was quite well suited to dedicated Fordist mass and flow production processes, although even there some flexibility had to be achieved by overtime arrangements, shift-working, etc. The flexibility now required is far greater.

This is one of the main factors underlying the spread of 'flexi-time', part-time work (Table 5.2) and other arrangements which increase the flexibility of the system as a whole. It is certainly not the only factor. Arguably the desire of many employees, especially women, to work part-time has been even more important. Supply and demand factors have interacted. The participation rate of women in the labour force has increased very rapidly in the last quarter century and has continued to rise in most cases through recessionary periods (Table 5.1). Self-employment has also risen (Tables 5.3 and 5.4) in some countries, especially the United Kingdom, but the rise in self-employment in services is offset by the continuing decline of self-employment in agriculture.

Lagging somewhat behind the changing attitudes of women, men too have been changing. According to surveys of women, the change has been very slow and incomplete. One such survey found that less than 5 per cent of men could be truly classified as 'new men', defined in this context as partners who were willing to take a truly equal share in child care and housework. However, a larger group (18 per cent) were designated as 'newish' men, i.e. men who were willing to do quite a lot, even though not as much as their partners. 'New' and 'newish' men were to be found mainly in the younger age groups. (MINTEL Survey, *The Times*, 21 Feb 1994)

Rather more objective evidence emerges from the time-budget surveys organised by Gershuny (1994) and other social scientists. These surveys show that typically in European countries over the period 1965–85 women spent less time in domestic work. About three-quarters of the decrease was accounted for by technical change

Table 5.2 Size and composition of part-time employment, 1973–1992 (%)

Part-time employment as a proportion of employment

	Men						Women					
	1973	1979	1983	1990	1991	1992	1973	1979	1983	1990	1991	1992
Australia	3.7	5.2	6.2	8.0	9.2	10.5	28.2	35.2	36.4	40.1	40.9	43.3
Austria	1.4	1.5	1.5	1.6	1.5	—	15.6	18.0	20.0	20.2	20.1	—
Belgium	1.0	1.0	2.0	2.0	2.1	—	10.2	16.5	19.7	25.8	27.4	—
Canada	4.7	5.7	7.6	8.1	8.8	9.3	19.4	23.3	26.1	24.4	25.5	25.9
Denmark	—	5.2	6.6	10.4	10.5	—	—	46.3	44.7	38.4	37.8	—
Finland	—	3.2	4.5	4.4	5.1	5.5	—	10.6	12.5	10.2	10.2	10.4
France	1.7	2.4	2.6	3.4	3.4	3.6	12.9	16.9	20.0	23.6	23.5	24.5
Germany	1.8	1.5	1.7	2.6	2.7	—	24.4	27.6	30.0	33.8	34.3	—
Greece	—	—	3.7	2.2	2.2	—	—	—	12.1	7.6	7.2	—
Ireland	—	2.1	2.7	3.4	3.6	—	14.0	13.1	15.5	17.6	17.8	—
Italy	3.7	3.0	2.4	2.4	2.9	2.7	25.1	10.6	9.4	9.6	10.4	10.5
Japan	6.8	7.5	7.3	9.5	10.1	10.6	18.4	27.8	29.8	33.4	34.3	34.8
Luxembourg	1.0	1.0	1.0	1.9	1.9	—	—	17.1	17.0	16.7	17.9	—
Netherlands^c	—	5.5	7.2	15.8	16.7	—	24.6	44.0	50.1	61.7	62.2	—
New Zealand	4.6	4.9	5.0	8.4	9.7	10.3	46.5	29.1	31.4	35.0	35.7	35.9
Norway^b	5.9	7.3	7.7	8.8	9.1	9.8	—	50.9	63.3	48.2	47.6	47.1
Portugal	—	2.5	—	3.6	4.0	4.2	—	16.5	—	10.1	10.5	11.0
Spain	—	—	—	1.6	1.5	2.0	—	—	—	11.8	11.2	13.7
Sweden^c	—	5.4	6.3	7.3	7.6	8.4	—	46.0	45.9	40.9	41.0	41.3
United Kingdom	2.3	1.9	3.3	5.3	5.5	6.1	39.1	39.0	42.4	43.2	43.7	44.6
United States	8.6	9.0	10.8	10.0	10.5	10.8	26.8	26.7	28.1	25.2	25.6	25.4

a Break in series after 1985.
b Break in series after 1987.
c Break in series after 1986.

Notes: The definition of part-time work varies considerably across OECD countries. Essentially three main approaches can be distinguished: i) a classification based on the worker's perception of his/her employment situation; ii) a cut-off (generally 30 or 35 hours per week based on usual working hours, with persons usually working less hours being considered part-timers; iii) a comparable cut-off based on actual hours worked during the reference week.

A criterion based on actual hours will generally yield a part-time rate higher than one based on usual hours, particularly if there are temporary reductions in working time as a result of holidays, illness, short-timing, etc. On the other hand, it is not entirely clear whether a classification based on the worker's perception will necessarily yield estimates of part-time work that are higher or lower than one based on a fixed cut-off. In one country (France) which changed from 1981 to 1982 from a definition based on an *actual* hours cut-off (30 hours) to one based on the respondent's perception, the latter criterion appeared to produce slightly higher estimates.

Other factors as well affect the international comparability of the estimates. In some countries, the hours cut-off is based on hours for the main job, in others on total hours for all jobs. Certain countries do not consider unpaid family workers to be employed unless they work more than a minimum number of hours, so that such workers do not enter into counts for part-time workers. The following describes the sources and definitions used for OECD countries, as well as the adjustments made by the Secretariat to ensure historical comparability.

Sources and definitions: Estimates for Belgium, Denmark, Germany, Greece, Ireland, Italy, Luxembourg, Portugal, Spain and the United Kingdom are from the annual Community Labour Force Survey and were obtained from *Labour Force Survey, Theme 3, Series C* (Eurostat) and from Commission sources. The part-time/full-time delineation is based on the respondent's own classification. Exceptions are Greece and Italy. For the former, a person is considered to be part-time if working fewer hours than stipulated in collective agreements applicable for the type of job at which the person is working. For Italy, a similar criterion is applied, i.e., a person works part-time if, in agreement with the employer, fewer than normal hours are worked in his/her particular type of employment.

Australia: Estimates are from the Labour Force Survey for the month of August (*The Labour Force Australia*, Australian Bureau of Statistics, catalogue No. 6203.0). Part-time workers are those who usually work less than 35 hours a week and who did so during the survey week. Prior to 1969, schoolteachers who usually worked less than 35 hours per week but who worked the full week during the reference week were considered part-time. They are now assimilated to full-time workers. Estimates prior to 1986 do not include unpaid family workers working less than 15 hours per week. No adjustments have been carried out for these breaks.

Source: OECD (1993).

Table 5.3 Number of self-employed persons (including agriculture) as a percentage of the total number of persons employed, 14 OECD countries, 1970, 1980, 1990

	1970	1980	1990
Australia	12.9	16.4	15.4
Belgium	19.1	16.4	17.9
Canada	11.6	9.8	9.7
Germany	16.6	11.7	10.6
Denmark	19.3	15.1	11.3
Finland	20.9	14.5	11.8
France	20.9	16.3	14.2
United Kingdom	7.8	7.9	12.6
Italy	30.7	30.2	31.5
Japan	33.6	26.6	20.0
Netherlands	15.7	13.0	12.3
Norway	17.4	12.7	10.6
Sweden	10.9	8.4	7.4
United States	9.1	9.0	8.0

Source: OECD.

Table 5.4 Number of self-employed persons (excluding agriculture) as a percentage of the total number of persons employed, 14 OECD countries, 1970, 1980, 1990*

	1970	1980	1990
Australia	8.6	13.0	12.6
Belgium	15.5	14.1	16.2
Canada	7.0	6.9	7.6
Germany	10.1	7.9	8.2
Denmark	12.0	9.8	7.9
Finland	6.3	4.8	5.5
France	12.1	10.2	10.0
United Kingdom	6.7	7.0	11.8
Italy	21.8	24.1	27.8
Japan	19.2	17.9	13.6
Netherlands	11.1	9.2	9.2
Norway	8.6	6.9	6.3
Sweden	6.3	5.2	5.3
United States	7.0	7.5	7.8

* For the United States 1990 is in fact 1989
Source: OECD.

(domestic appliances, etc.) but a quarter was compensated by a rise in male contributors to child care and domestic work. From the standpoint of men, even amongst the older age groups many could be found who regretted that they were not able to spend more time with their young children. Often they would have liked to do so but were constrained by the inflexibility of working-time arrangements and career pressures as well as the attitudes of their employers. It should be as easy for a father to get time to look after a sick child as for a mother, or to meet the children after school and care for them. But in practice, it is often far more difficult for fathers even when they very much want to take this time off. Flexibility of working hours is thus increasingly important for men as well as for women, and not only for 'new men' but for 'old' men too, even though simple biological differences mean that the division of labour can never be quite the same. The 'Parenting Deficit' identified by Etzioni (1993) and other sociologists as a key social problem can only be reduced if this type of flexibility improves.

Much has been written about these trends in working hours and part-time work, both by labour economists and by sociologists and management theorists. One of the most interesting and provocative recent studies is that of Hewitt (1993) in her book *About Time: The Revolution in Work and Family Life*. She argues that although traditional working-time arrangements have been eroded in many ways, they still represent a formidable barrier to flexibility in working time, hindering the emergence of a new pattern which could match the changing needs of both employers and employees. In her view this new pattern would involve shorter working hours for those now in full-time employment but full- or part-time work would be available for all those who wished to contribute. The Report on Social Cohesion prepared by Holland (1993) for the EU also advocates reduced working hours and estimates that 8 or 9 million new jobs could be generated in the EU by this means by the year 2002 (p. 49).

Such a reduction in working hours could apply to weekly, annual and life-time hours. Charles Handy (1989) has estimated that lifetime working hours have fallen from about 100,000 for his generation to 50,000 for his children, whilst a slightly more precise calculation by Bruce Williams (1984) estimated the decline in lifetime working hours in Britain as 42 per cent from 1881 to 1981 (from 154,000 hours to 88,000 hours). Handy suggested that typically those who worked 100,000 hours did 47 hours a week for 47 weeks a year, for 47 years of employment, whereas today typical patterns could be for 50,000 hours made up from a 37-hour week for 37 weeks of 37 years, or 45 hours for 45 weeks for 25 years (early retirement and long education), or 25 hours for 45 weeks for 45 years (continuous part-time work). The slow decline of annual working hours continued in the 1980s (Table 5.5) but there are some slight indications of a reversal at least for some groups in the most recent period.

Hewitt insists that there should be a very wide variety of working hours which would not necessarily conform precisely to any of the above patterns. She argues that this is the actual trend of events and not just wishful thinking. Among the various possibilities she mentions are flexi-time, the nine-day fortnight, special leave for new parents (men and women), part-time working before and after retirement, job-sharing, longer working day with shorter working week, weekend jobs, annual hours contracts, zero hours contracts (work 'as and when required'), individually contracted working hours, career breaks, and sabbaticals. All of these have been spreading according to the evidence which she presents. Government authorities have quite often been ready to introduce part-time working arrangements for some of their own civil servants (Table 5.6). However, some of the most flexible schemes are to be found in the private sector. For example, B&Q, a part of the Kingfisher Group with 279 DIY stores in Britain and 15,000 employees, has 55 per cent of its workers working permanent part-time (of whom 70 per cent are women). Sixteen per cent work

Table 5.5 Average hours actually worked per person per year[a]

	1970	1973	1975	1979	1983	1990	1991	1992
Total employment								
Canada	1890	1865	1837	1794	1730	1733	1713	1709
Finland	1982	1915	1885	1859	1798	1756	1758	1728
France	1962	1904	1865	1813	1711	1669	1667	1666
Italy	1969	1885	1841	1788	1764	—	—	—
Japan	—	2185	2100	2110	2081	2023	—	—
Norway	1766	1694	1653	1501	1471	1415	1408	1417
Spain	—	—	—	2148	2052	1941	1931	1911
Sweden	1641	1557	1516	1451	1453	1480	1468	1485
United States	1886	1875	1833	1808	1788	1782	1771	1769
Dependent employment								
France	1821	1771	1720	1667	1558	1539	1540	1542
Germany	1885	1804	1737	1699	1670	1573	1557	—
Netherlands	—	—	—	1591	1530	1433	1423	—
Spain	—	—	—	2032	1946	1858	1847	1828
United States	1836	1831	1791	1767	1754	1749	1737	1736

[a] Includes part-time work.

Sources:
Canada: Data supplied by Statistics Canada.
Finland: Data estimated from National Accounts data.
France: Data supplied by INSEE on a National Accounts basis.
Germany: Data supplied by the German Institut für Arbeitsmarkt- und Berufsforschung.
Italy: Data supplied by the Italian authorities (ISTAT).
Japan: Secretariat estimates based on data from the *Monthly Labour Survey of Establishments* and the *Labour Force Survey*.
Netherlands: Data are annual contractual hours on the basis of Labour Accounts data and were supplied by the national authorities (CBS).
Norway: Data supplied by the Central Bureau of Statistics.
Spain: Data estimated from the quarterly *Labour Force Survey*.
Sweden: Data estimated from National Accounts data.
United States: Data provided by the Bureau of Labor Statistics.

Saturdays only, 14 per cent Sundays while the hours of other part-time workers vary according to the needs of the local store and of the individuals concerned. Some work mornings only, others in the afternoon, some a mixture of the two. All employees get the same basic hourly rate, company bonus and profit share regardless of hours but only those working 16 hours a week or more qualify for pension scheme membership. Surveys apparently show a high level of work satisfaction from these arrangements.

As Hewitt recognises, there are some dangers in the trend which she observes towards flexible part-time working. She is concerned that social security arrangements in particular are lagging behind the speed of change and that whilst some employers, such as B&Q, may make relatively good schemes, others may use the change simply to

Table 5.6 Part-time opportunities for civil servants

Country	Eligibility	Hours	Pay/conditions	Return to full-time	Duration
Australia	All with 3 mths service	15–30	Pro rata	Right to return after agreed period	By agreement
Austria	Women with children 1–4 All caring for close relative	Half-time	—	"	1 or 2 yrs; 4 yrs total
Belgium	Permanent civil servants with family/social needs; for personal convenience	50%–80% normal hrs	Pro rata	"	3 mths–2 yrs at one time; 5 yrs total
Canada	All	Minimum 1/3 normal hrs	Pro rata	—	—
France	All	50%–90% normal hrs	Pro rata	"	6 mths minimum
Germany	All with child below 18 or dependent adult	Minimum 50% normal hrs	—	With permission	Up to 15 yrs
Italy	All; limit on total part-time posts			Pro rata	—	—
Luxembourg	All with child below 15 or 'well motivated' personal reasons; very senior posts excluded	Half-time	Minimum 50% normal hrs	Only if full-time vacancy	No limit
New Zealand	All, for personal reasons	—	Pro rata for pensions: does not count towards promotion	—	—
Portugal	All with 3 yrs service, with children under 12, sick relative or educational needs; except directorate or executive positions	Half-time	Pro rata	Right to return on request	6 mths; can be extended
Sweden	All	Compatible with service	Pro rata	—	No limit
USA	All up to grade GS-16	16–32 hours	Pro rata	—	—

Source: ILO (1989); Hewitt (1993).

— Indicates no information given.

avoid their responsibilities to employees. The 1994 legal decision of the House of Lords on the application of EU legislation to British part-time workers will have some countervailing effects.

In the absence of a strong overall demand for labour, the spread of part-time work could be largely involuntary (see Figure 7.1 in the final chapter). The very real dangers to work morale were pointed out in an editorial in *The Economist* (17 July 1993):

Challenged by nimbler rivals, big firms have little choice but to slim down. Many are still too bureaucratic and need to shed yet more workers. With competition increasing, firms of every size must react more quickly. But bosses are wrong to believe that the best way to do this is to tear up the implicit contract they have had with their employees. At pre-sent too many firms are trying to heap all of the uncertainty created by increased competition and technological change upon the shoulders of individual workers. There are limits to how far firms can adopt this approach if they hope to remain competitive beyond the shortest of short terms.

When recession ends, western firms will find that retaining good employees and motivating mediocre ones is far more difficult. Worried about their next job or career-switch, workers will not care much about any firm's long-term fortunes unless given good reason to do so. To suc-ceed, bosses will need to reach a new understanding with employees. The Japanese system is too alien to import wholesale. Turning the clock back and offering the prospect of a 40-year climb up the career ladder will be impossible. With the message of constant change drummed into them, no one will believe such a promise.

Instead, firms will be forced to experiment with new employment pat-terns that accommodate the needs of skilled, middle-class workers as well as the firms' own wants. Job-sharing, sabbaticals, subsidised education, flexible hours, telecommuting, creches, paternity as well as maternity leave — today's frills will become the ingredients of any new under-standing between employees and companies. Bosses may not be able to offer continuous advancement, or even employment. But they can offer flexibility, and a commitment to rehire as soon as possible workers who leave or are laid off.

Most people may be willing to accept the prospect of variable pay-for-performance, interrupted employment and constant retraining. But they are seeking in return firms ready to take into account the needs of single parents and two-career couples, issues which many bosses have barely even thought about. Such indifference is costly. In the workplace of the future, the fiercest competition between firms may not be for customers, but for the hearts and minds of employees.

This warning from *The Economist* on the dangers to the firm's long-term competitiveness from neglect of human capital is supported by a study at the OECD, which shows that formal company training is more limited in countries where labour turnover is high. For example, in the United States only 10 per cent of young recruits had any formal training from their company, compared with around 70 per cent in Japan and Germany. The OECD study concludes that there is a clear link between employment stability and skill training. Short-term competitive advantage to the firm could be at the expense of structural competitiveness to the nation. We turn now to consider the role of skills and human capital in promoting flexibility.

5.4 Flexibility and skills

The growth and decline of employment opportunities is not limited to the growth and decline of sectors. A particular feature of the rise in structural unemployment over the last two decades is the growing educational and occupational 'mismatch' between job losses and new employment opportunities — as Sherman and Jenkins (1979) put it, 'how to tell a redundant Scottish steel worker that there is a job opportunity as a secretary in London'. The labour market is from this perspective an extremely heterogeneous 'market' which does not adjust to incentives in the same immediate way as financial markets would. Many of the structural changes associated with changes in the demand for new skills and qualifications are directly the result of technological change.

In Chapter 3 we discussed some of the consequences of the ICT techno-economic paradigm for work organisation and flexibility. These have been conveniently summarised and presented by Boyer (1989), as shown in Table 5.7. From this it is clear that the problems of 'mismatch' in the skills of the work-force arise not just from changes in the sectoral composition of output and of the labour force but also from changes *within* each enterprise (Boyer and Caroli, 1993).

The rise of the computer industry, of telecommunication networks, of various electronic capital goods and consumer goods, of software and related information services, and the decline of employment in some more traditional heavy industries, such as steel and coal, do of course in themselves cause major problems of structural unemployment. To continue the Jenkins and Sherman example: it is often easier for the *wives* of unemployed steel-workers and miners to get jobs in the new industries and services than it is for the men themselves. Geographical concentration of the older heavy industries may often aggravate these problems. The sectoral shifts in employment which

Table 5.7 From Fordism to a new model: a synoptic presentation

Fordist principles	The challenges of the 1970s and 1980s	Principles of a new model
F1: Rationalisation of labour is the main target, mechanisation is the means	C1: Underutilisation of equipment, large inventories of work in process	P1: Global optimisation of productive flows
F2: First design and then manufacture and organise work process	C2: Delays and large costs in passing from innovation to effective production	P2: Tentative full integration of research, development and production
F3: Indirect and mediated links with consumers via marketing studies and strategies	C3: Losing touch with choosy consumers, failures in launching new products	P3: Close and long-lasting ties between producers and users, capture learning by using effects
F4: Low cost for standardised products is the first objective, quality the second one	C4: *Ex-post* quality controls cannot prevent a rising defect rate, consumers more selective about quality	P4: High quality at reasonable costs, via a zero-defect objective, at each stage of the production process
F5: Mass production for stable and rising demands, batch production for unstable demands	C5: Even mass consumer demand becomes uncertain: the Fordist production process appears rigid	P5: Insert the market demand into the production process, in order to get fast responses
F6: Centralisation of most decisions about production in a special division of a large firm	C6: Sluggish and inadequate reaction of headquarters to global and local shocks	P6: Decentralisation as far as possible of production decisions within smaller and less hierarchical units
F7: Vertical integration, mitigated by circles of subcontractors	C7: Given radical innovations, even large firms can no longer master all the techniques needed for their core business	P7: Networking (and joint ventures), as a method for reaping both specialisation and coordination gains

F8: Facing cyclical demand, subcontractors are used as stabilising device, in order to preserve large firms' employment	C8: During the 1970s, bankruptcies and/or loss of competence of subcontractors, now confronted with international competition	P8: Long-run and cooperative subcontracting as far as possible in order to promote joint technical innovations
F9: Divide and specialise at most productive tasks, main source of productivity increases	C9: Excessive labour division might turn counterproductive: rising control and monitoring costs; built-in rigidity	P9: To recompose production, maintenance, quality control and some management tasks might be more efficient, technically and economically
F10: Minimise the required general education and on-the-job training of productive tasks according to Babbage's and Taylor's principles	C10: New technical opportunities (IT), more competition and uncertain demands challenge most of the previous specialised tasks	P10: A new alliance between a minimal general education and effective on-the-job training, in order to maximise individual and collective competence
F11: Hierarchical control and purely financial incentives to manufacture an implicit consent to poor job content	C11: Young generations, better educated and with different expectations, reject authoritarian management styles. Too much control becomes counterproductive	P11: Human resources policies have to spur workers' competence and commitment and work out positive support for firm's strategy
F12: Adversarial industrial relations converge towards wage demands; collective agreements codify a provisional armistice	C12: Firms' employment might be hurt by the lack of cooperation and an exclusive concern for wages. On the other hand, concession bargaining does not necessarily provide any advantage for wage-earners	P12: An explicit and long-term compromise between managers and wage earners is needed to reap a general support for this model: commitment vs. good working conditions and/or job tenures and/or a fair sharing of modernisation dividends

Source: Boyer (1989), modified by J. Bengtsson, (1993).

have been summarised in Chapter 4 together with the changes in the skill composition of the work-force in almost *every* sector lead to the following aggregate effects.

(1) A continuation of the long-term trend towards an increased proportion of 'information workers' in total employment. This trend existed already long before computerisation and was analysed by sociologists such as Daniel Bell (1974) and economists such as Machlup (1962). However, an increasing proportion of these 'information workers' will need good communication skills and at least elementary computing skills. Flexibility in firms and in governments and in networks of firms will increasingly depend on the almost universal availability of these skills. Whereas the classical economists could often think in terms of unskilled (and often illiterate) manual labour as a universal interchangeable equivalent, and Marx could think in terms of an 'industrial reserve army' of unemployed to impart flexibility and discipline to the system, today this flexibility depends on a work-force with a good general level of education and some basic skills in handling, processing and transmitting information. Discipline within the work-force depends increasingly on understanding, participation and communication rather than simply the threat of the sack or other penalties. This too depends on good general education as well as firm-based training and retraining at all levels of the work-force.

(2) Universal literacy was of course already useful for previous technology systems but in fact many firms operated with a high proportion of the work-force which was only semi-literate as well as innumerate. This was the case even in countries with universal primary and secondary education, such as the United States. It was graphically illustrated when firms such as Motorola had to introduce successively more complex generations of new products in their many factories across the United States. Wiggenhorn (1990) has described in the *Harvard Business Review* how the company discovered that their work-force needed remedial primary and secondary education as well as more graduates and specialised skills in order to reach the quality standards which are now essential. Motorola was led to develop a company education and training programme in collaboration with primary, secondary and tertiary educational institutions in more than thirty states where it had manufacturing and other establishments. Nor is this case atypical. *The Financial Times* (16 February 1994) reported the results of a survey which showed that 92 per cent of British employers reported insufficient command of the English

language while 38 per cent had to spend money on training to bring recruits' literacy to the standard required. These and similar surveys in other countries show the need for big improvements in the *quality* of general education, particularly to upgrade the performance of the low achievers who do not always fit into the present pattern of classroom learning and examinations. For example, the thorough international comparative studies by Prais and his colleagues (1987, 1989) show that this is one of the main weaknesses of the British education and training system. Whereas this problem is often represented as one of a return to older educational ideas of learning by rote, classroom discipline and standardised curricula, we shall argue in Chapter 7 that information technology itself (through multi-media systems, CD-ROMs, virtual reality, etc.) now offers the best hope of a drastic improvement in the quality of education by providing pupil-based and pupil-paced learning facilities of an imaginative kind in every discipline and vocation.

(3) Although raising the general universal standard of literacy and numeracy is essential to enhance flexibility, it has to be complemented, of course, by intensive education and training for specialised skills, especially those related to ICT. We have already argued in Chapter 3 that, contrary to the pessimistic views sometimes put forward, there will in fact be an enormously increased need for software designers and engineers. They will be needed not least to achieve the objective just mentioned of raising the quality of education and training throughout the system. But they will also be needed for numerous other applications of computer systems, such as telecommunication networks, data banks, tele-conferencing, traffic control, monitoring of arms control agreements, many types of R&D, etc., etc. However, whereas computer hardware and software professionals are at the heart of the ICT revolution, there is also a parallel though less intense need for many other professionally qualified people in natural science, engineering, social sciences, medicine, management and humanities. Although there are conflicting views and there is a possibility of alternative patterns of evolution in different countries, the main trend which is being driven by the ICT revolution appears to be towards a generally higher level of both specialised skills and general education with a declining share in future work-force composition both for unskilled and for lower-qualified workers. To some extent of course this evolution depends on the policies which are adopted and we have argued that for many

reasons to compete with higher skills is more desirable than to adjust downwards to compete in low-skill, low-wage activities. It is to the policies needed to implement this goal that we turn in Chapter 7, but first we discuss some problems of the transition to a less polluting technology system in Chapter 6.

5.5 Conclusions

In this chapter we have discussed several aspects of 'flexibility' and we do believe that greater flexibility can contribute to structural adjustment. However, flexibility is certainly not an end in itself and some degree of predictability and stability is also essential in any economy. Physical infrastructures and human settlement patterns provide a 'vertebrate' structure for any economy without which it would be difficult to sustain any ordered pattern of growth or confidence in future investment decisions. As we have already argued in Chapter 3, institutions are not simply a source of inertia and resistance to novelty. Paradoxically, they are actually essential for innovation itself. A purely 'invertebrate' economy would be one in which it would be impossible to form any stable expectations. The problem for the transition from one techno-economic paradigm to another is not therefore one of introducing infinite flexibility. Rather is it one of reducing rigidity in some areas while introducing greater stability and a stronger regulatory and legal framework in others — for example, in relation to standards.

With respect to employment this could mean that the need for increased flexibility in occupational patterns, skill profiles, work organisation and work time may have to be combined with a search for new structures, new 'rigidities' which make it workable for individuals to invest in education, training and the acquisition of new skills. The institutional rigidity of 'life-long' employment in the large Japanese enterprises was instrumental to the high skill and occupational mobility *within* such enterprises. It is not possible simply to transfer the Japanese model to other countries with quite different institutions and traditions. However, it does illustrate the point that great flexibility in one direction can be combined with strong vertebrate structures in others. Ideally, Europe should strive for such prolonged conditions of full employment that people would readily accept the need for considerable flexibility in reskilling and retraining for occupational mobility. In the next chapter we discuss 'sustainable development' which in our view would mean some rather stable long-term expectations about the future in a rather 'vertebrate' economy.

Notes

[1]   It is, however, interesting to observe that *internal* migration has declined with further European integration, whereas it is the *external* migration pressures which have increased.

[2]   It could well be claimed that Kalecki developed his own version of 'Keynesian' employment theory simultaneously or even earlier.

[3]   We do not discuss here the various policy proposals directed at reductions in labour costs, while leaving wages intact. Proposals at shifting the tax burden away from labour towards other inputs such as materials or energy are undisputed. Their uncoordinated implementation in individual European countries appears though difficult, because of fears of losing international competitiveness. We come back to this issue in Chapter 7.

6

SUSTAINABLE DEVELOPMENT AND LIMITS TO
GROWTH: the end of the love affair with the
automobile

6.1 Introduction

As emphasized in Chapters 2 and 3, the emergence of new technologies such as ICT today or previous 'technological juggernauts' centred around cheap oil, petro-chemicals, plastics, automobiles and consumer durables has fundamentally transformed economic production, consumption, our way of life and the international mobility of goods and persons. The discussion on the employment impact of such radical change is part of a much wider and broader debate about both the positive and the negative 'externalities' of such radical change: benefiting many but often to the detriment of some. Thus, while technological progress in the post-war period has led to unprecedented prosperity, at least in the Western industrialised countries, the burdens on the lives of some groups of individuals have often been high.

The *environmental*, long-term, negative 'externalities' problems of past industrialisation and application of technology, such as the use of pesticides, new chemicals and synthetic materials, and the continuous flow of hazardous emissions, effluent and waste material do, however, not only affect the lives of individuals in some areas or countries; they also affect the welfare of future generations — in some cases at the level of the entire world. These environmental 'externalities' often go unnoticed or even undetected for a very long time.

Unlike past technological 'externalities', our awareness of our current environmental problems stems from the accumulation of small effects, which at some point in time appear to exceed the critical boundaries of the eco-system or at least our perception of those boundaries. They represent in other words a typical example of an evolutionary process in which small events can develop into a much larger, intricate and complex problem over a longer period of time. The environmental 'externalities' of growth could be viewed as the dark side of the rise of Fordist mass-production industry: a slow and gradual 'locking-in' into a less and less efficient networking system, whereby congestion and environmental costs are gradually increasing.

In this chapter we discuss the particular contribution the emergence and further diffusion of the ICT techno-economic paradigm might make to the development and ultimate attainment of an environmentally sustainable economic development. In doing so our analysis contains of course a number of speculative arguments. However, these are based on what we would maintain are valid historical analogies as well as on our own analysis in Chapter 3 of the potentialities of new ICT. The substitution of communication and more knowledge-based activities for some present-day polluting activities and the potential for better control and measurement of environmental costs are both essential for the development of economic incentives and adjustments away from environmental degradation.

In the next section we briefly discuss the notion of externalities of technological change. That notion is well recognized in the 'technology assessment' (TA) literature but has too often been overlooked by economists. Technological change just like any other form of change may bring benefits to most of us but often if not always at the cost of some. Sometimes those costs, however, appear hidden and the benefits of today are in striking contrast with the sometimes huge costs to future generations. In the following section we elaborate, albeit briefly, on the basis of historical analogy on the transition towards a more sustainable growth path which ICT might represent. Finally in the last two sections we broaden this analysis to international mobility and the future role of trade in goods and services along this new environmentally sustainable growth and development path.

While we are rather outspoken with respect to the role of ICT in bringing about such a growth bifurcation in the direction of a more environmentally sustainable development path, we are less explicit about the likely employment implications of such a development path. We enter a little more explicitly into the discussion of possible future employment opportunities in Chapter 7.

6.2 The 'externalities' of technological change

For a long time economists have recognised that the purely internal calculations within each firm of their own costs and benefits may not take into account important external effects of their actions. This gave rise to the technique known as cost–benefits analysis designed to measure these social costs and benefits. TA ('technology assessment') is in many respects simply an extension of this type of analysis and it is now relatively well established in the debate surrounding technology policy. It has emerged as a part of the democratic parliamentary institutional set up in the United States and many other developed countries precisely because of the recognition of the 'externality' nature of much technical change and the danger of disenfranchising all but a few experts. It appeared that a well-informed assessment of new technologies could provide some reassurance about likely impacts or even shape it in a way that is desired. By definition, though, TA can address much better what we will call here the static distributional aspects of the impact of technology than the dynamic externality aspects.

First, from a *static* point of view, and as emphasized in particular by Harvey Brooks (1973), there is a distributional paradox regarding the impact of technology. The costs or risks of a new technology frequently fall on a limited group of the population — as exemplified in the case of employment displacement and the scrapping of old skills — whereas the benefits are often widely diffused; sometimes the benefits to any restricted group are barely perceptible even though the aggregate benefit to a large population amounts to considerably more than the total cost to the limited adversely affected group. The employment impact of new technologies is a typical example. 'Automation', for instance, may benefit consumers of a product by lowering its relative price, but the costs in worker displacement are borne by a small number of people, and may be traumatic. A large electricity generating station may adversely affect the local environment, while providing widely diffused benefits to the population served by the electricity produced. Workers in an unusually dangerous occupation such as mining carry a disproportionate share of the costs associated with the mined minerals which may have wide benefits throughout a national economy.

This disproportion between costs and benefits can, however, also work the other way as in many cases of environmental pollution and emissions. The effluents from a concentrated industrial area such as the Walloon industrial area along the Meuse or the Ruhr Valley along the Rhine will diffuse various pollutants over a very large surrounding area which derives little benefit from the industrial activity, but may suffer severe environmental degradation.

The problems of sharing such costs and benefits of technological change have shown how important it is, both from a national and international perspective, to draw up 'rules of the game' to ensure that adverse effects are less harmful than they would be if everything was left to free competition; and, second, to establish such rules fairly early on, before vested interests or the fierceness of competition jeopardise their compulsory application. The discussion parallels here some of the discussion on the international dimension of technical change and in particular the 'negative' adjustment or flexibility induced by international competition.

Undoubtedly, though, the biggest challenge posed by environmental externalities of technical change relates to possible *dynamic* externalities. Within a dynamic, evolutionary perspective, such long-term externalities are, in Nelson and Winter's (1982) words, no longer

susceptible to definitive once and for all categorization and are more intimately related to particular historical and institutional contexts. To a large extent, the problems involved are aspects of economic change. The processes of change are continually tossing up new 'externalities' that must be dealt with in some manner or other. In a regime in which technical advance is occurring and organizational structure is evolving in response to changing patterns of demand and supply, new non-market interactions that are not contained adequately by prevailing laws and policies are almost certain to appear, and old ones may disappear. Long lasting chemical insecticides were not a problem eighty years ago. Horse manure polluted the cities but automotive emissions did not. The canonical 'externality' problem of evolutionary theory is the generation by new technologies of benefits and costs that old institutional structures ignore. (p. 368)

The environmental problems and threats the world is facing, such as the destruction of the ozone layer and global warming, imply that present institutional regimes are to a large extent inadequate. Automotive emissions are now a major problem. Until now use or abuse of the environment has been regulated, if at all, by emission norms, product standards and bans, and — in some cases — charges and subsidies. These measures have been largely insufficient because they have only led to the development and use of 'cleaning' technology such as 'end-of-pipe' technology and other treatment technology instead of 'clean' technology (cleaner production processes) through which environmental damage could ultimately be prevented (Kemp and Soete, 1992).

The broad array of present environmental policy debates over some of the long-term externalities of change, including technological change, in terms of impact on the physical global environment (air, land and water pollution), or even in terms of impact on society's future genetic capital (genetic manipulation, pre-embryo research), are in other words all part of the same need for a continuous reassessment of long-term costs and benefits of change and the accompanying need for institutional adaptation and experimentation. Confronted with an increasing amount of negative environmental externalities of past growth and change, governments are faced with a major challenge. How to define and develop the state's function as long-term — as opposed to short-term — social regulator of change in a period not only characterised by an increasingly international environment, but also by continuous new discoveries — some real, others perceived — of long-term negative environmental externalities of growth and change?

It is within this context that ICT as a new, pervasive and possibly environmentally friendly techno-economic paradigm takes on its particular significance.

6.3 The transition of technological growth paths: from motor vehicles to electronics

As discussed in more detail in Chapter 3 with respect to ICT, but argued more extensively in some previous work (Freeman et al., 1982; Freeman and Soete, 1987), economic growth is likely to be characterised by clusters of economically interrelated technological trajectories, which can be described as new techno-economic paradigms (Perez, 1983, 1985; Freeman and Perez, 1988). The network of technological trajectories related to cheap oil-based energy, combined with mass production and utilisation of the automobile as a cheap individualised transport system, can be said to have characterized the postwar period of rapid growth. In a similar fashion, other networks (e.g. electricity) have been identified with respect to previous periods of rapid growth (see Chapter 3).

As each system of 'network' infrastructure grows and develops further, side by side with positive externalities, more and more negative externalities often associated with the saturation of the network are likely to occur. Congestion, nuisance of all kinds, etc. will gradually increase, so that the growth trajectory will eventually reach its limits. Canals in the eighteenth and nineteenth centuries are a good example, as is horse transport in inner cities at the end of this century. From such a perspective, we would argue that present environmental problems signal in a similar way to earlier congestion problems the limits of the particular growth trajectory. A brief historical analogy might clarify the point we are trying to make.

At the end of the last century the city of London was facing enormous congestion and environmental problems related to the use of horses as a means of transport. A visual representation of the size of this congestion problem is given in Figure 6.1. However, what the visual picture does not illustrate is the particular environmental problems such a 'horse-dependent' transport system brought with it. It is estimated that horses produce no less than 15 kilos of manure per day. Most street corners in the city of London were patrolled by so-called crossing sweepers, whose task was not to keep the roads clean, but to clear the way for pedestrians. At the end of the nineteenth century there were around six thousand crossing sweepers in London. Alternative means of transport had been available for years, but were little used because of restrictive regulations and lack of appropriate infrastructure. The small-scale production restricted the realisation of dynamic learning and scale effects, and the lack of infrastructure facilities (electricity generation, gasoline stations, garages, etc.) prevented network externalities from arising. In relation to horses, cars had a level of about 200 times fewer emissions and waste (measured in grams per mile) (Montrol and Badger, 1974, p. 224). How much this contributed to the eventual disappearance of the horse as a means of transport and the rapid development and diffusion of underground railways, automobiles and electric trams (Grübler, 1990) can be left to historians. What we do know is that the growth bifurcation that took place became feasible in environmental terms.

The parallel with today's environmental transport problem is striking. Quite apart from public transport systems, the alternative ICT technological development trajectory is of course known and has been available for quite some time, typified by the replacement of car commuter traffic by fully interactive telecommunication systems, allowing for activities like home-work, tele-shopping, home-banking, etc. These alternatives have been available in most Western countries for several years as often locally applied technological experiments, but without having much success. Even the broadband telecommuni-

Figure 6.1 Traffic at Ludgate Circus, 1870

Source: G. Dore (1872), *Impressions of London*, London, Blanchard Jerold. (Reproduced in Montrol and Badger (1974), p. 228.)

cation systems, which have been highly praised, have actually been slow to diffuse. The reasons for this are similar to those given in the previous example: unforeseen and inappropriate regulations (e.g. the status of home workers); the size of the infrastructural facilities required (e.g. initial required costs attached to an interactive electronic network); the problem of acceptable standards, the wide range of institutional and infrastructural adjustments and facilities (e.g. the eventual need for a complete transformation of ideas related to the localisation of work; the replanning of cities; the new role of leisure time, etc.).[1] The reorganisation of households to accommodate the necessary ICT equipment raises problems analogous to the redesign of kitchens to accommodate domestic appliances but the problem of who should bear the costs is more complicated. Early studies have shown considerable disillusion and aggravation of family tensions in tele-working households. (Haddon and Silverstone, 1994).

In other words, in some cases alternative technological 'network' possibilities do exist and are available. They do, however, as in the present case, face major barriers because the 'positive' growth and employment creation externalities involved can only develop over time and are prevented from doing so by the existing dominant institutional framework. Their diffusion is in our view essential for an effective growth bifurcation to take place: growth based less on the highly inefficient individualised transport system of persons than on the far more efficient transportation of information and both new and older forms of public transport.

Of course, the present-day environmental problems and risks are much broader and involve much more than gasoline emissions and the danger of overexploitation of fossil energy sources. The example above signals, however, a more fundamental point; it is not so much economic growth as such that is not sustainable in terms of the environment but rather particular technological and economic growth paths that are not sustainable. As one of us put it in the Limits to Growth debate, 'the mistake of the MIT modellers (and some of the Marxists) was to confuse the 'limits' of a particular development paradigm with the limits to growth of the system in general' (Freeman, 1984, p. 499).

Thus, what is needed is a change in the 'techno-economic paradigm', in the 'ecological modernisation', based on principles of sustainable development, i.e. the closing of chains of materials, energy savings and cleaner processes and products. This change in the techno-economic paradigm involves a wide array of changes in industry, transportation and agriculture. It involves the substitution of certain hazardous substances and materials such as CFCs, asbestos and dangerous pesticides, the reduction of harmful emissions and the reduction and recycling of waste material, and the 'enabling' of new infrastructure technologies (telecommunication, public transport). Insight into the market stimuli, the technological opportunities and the possibilities of redirecting technological advance is of great importance.

6.3 From GATTpeace to Greenpeace: on trade, mobility and transport costs

Undoubtedly the dramatic improvements in transport technology have been behind much of the economic growth process over the post-war period. Even before then, as Figure 6.2 illustrates, the combination of major advances and switches in transport systems as well as the gradual expansion of alternative transport network systems have provided the essential basis for growth and development since the industrial revolution. As Kondratieff (1925) himself suggested, investment in new infrastructures is a major factor in the long cycles which bear his name.

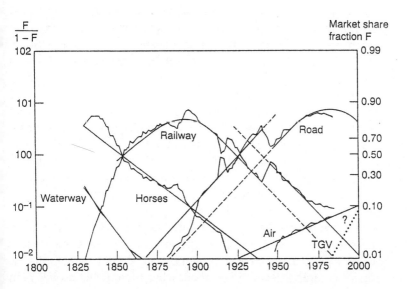

Figure 6.2 Modal split in passenger (intra- and intercity) transport in France, in fractional share of passenger/km performed, logit transformation

Source: Grübler (1990).

The gradual expansion of those networks has been accompanied, as illustrated in Figure 6.2, by a gradual saturation of such transport systems, leading finally to the partial or total replacement of one system with another, more efficient transport system. This has not just been the case with respect to canals and horse-dependent transport systems being replaced with railways; it has also been the case with the gradual replacement of railways with road and air-dependent traffic in the post-war period. With respect to these two latter systems one might argue that here too one is now gradually entering saturation.

That saturation is actually enhanced by two apparently contradictory but similar trends. The first can be seen in the continuing technological improvements in motor car technology and in particular in the fuel efficiency of combustion engines, leading to a lower cost of transport (this could be considered as similar to the 'sailing ship' effect whereby at the end of last century improvements in sailing technology allowed sailing ships to remain competitive, at least in terms of speed with steam-powered ships). While many of these improvements have been inspired by the rise in oil prices and in particular the second oil shock and more recently environmental concerns, their widespread diffusion has actually been accompanied by a decline in the real price of oil, thus further reducing the cost of motor car transport. Second, the particular features of the individualised and completely flexible motor car transport mode have given this transport system the aura of entertainment or costless, 'free' time. Some consumers are readily prepared to consider travel time in their personal motor cars as entertainment, or part of their free time, a form of escape or even as a mobile cottage or work-place. The acceptable levels of time wasted in traffic jams appears as a consequence extremely elastic. As a result consumers do not calculate rationally their costs of mobility. Potential new technologies which could substitute for this mobility such as ICT (as in the case of teleworking) will rather be used as in Carlota Perez's case of the electric toothbrush with respect to electricity, as complementary technologies, allowing even greater mobility (as in the case of the mobile phone, fax, etc.): the car with driver as the mobile office.

A similar trend can be observed with respect to freight transport and tourism. Alongside similar energy efficiency improvements and expansion of existing transport networks, one should also emphasise the role of container technology in allowing the interaction between sea, canal, rail and road transport systems. Container technology has been essential in the rapid growth of international trade flows in the post-war period. The dramatic growth in air freight transport is similarly based on improvements in fast interactions with other transport modes. While air transport has taken over as transport mode for valuable manufactured goods, as illustrated in Figure 6.3, it has also increasingly allowed for light-weight, highly time-dependent goods such as flowers in the Dutch case. Similar considerations apply to the Fordist packaged holidays and airline reservation systems (Poon, 1993).

What these trends in technological improvements hide, however, is the growing environmental cost of such increased mobility, both of persons and goods. In particular, with respect to the environmental transport costs in international trade, few economists have looked at such costs. We would argue that these might well be higher than the conventional gains from trade in many cases, particularly when there is no environmental policy aimed at reducing pollution introduced in the trading countries, or in the countries which solely benefit from the cross-border trade (see the debates in Austria and Switzerland about cross-border EU trade from Germany to Italy or France).

In the economic literature the result that conventional gains from trade may be outweighed by losses from increased pollution has come to be acknowledged, but only in the case when such pollution is

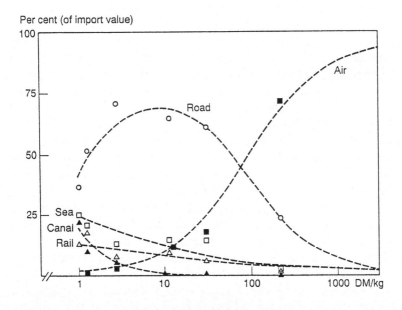

Figure 6.3 Share of different transport modes in the value of imported manufactured goods vs. value density of products in the FRG, 1986 (per cent of import value vs. average product value in DM/kg)

Source: Grübler (1990).

directly related to output production. However, such analyses ignore many of the pollution costs associated with the actual transport of commodities. In the case of air freight transport, these have been shown to be substantial. Furthermore, there are, because of international conventions regulating air transport, no taxes on kerosene, the common air fuel. As a result international mobility and transport costs have been kept artificially low and bear no relation to the actual environmental 'externalities'.

In so far as specialisation, whether within the national boundaries of a country or at the broader international level, is at the core of much of the developed and industrialising world's economic growth, because of the improved allocation of resources and the reaping of advantages associated with increasing returns to scale, the ignorance of the transport environmental costs associated with such specialisation might well have led to an overemphasis of the positive externalities of such change, even in the environmental sphere. Thus, the reaping of scale advantages might have been accompanied by increased emissions and other negative environmental externalities as a result of the increased transport flows even if emission costs might have been reduced at the point of production.

From this perspective, one might argue that, as in the extreme case of air transport but also with respect to many other transport systems, there has been a general subsidisation of transport and mobility more generally, whether such systems are publicly or privately run, and whether of a national or international nature. In the case of current dominant transport systems such as road and air, there is little doubt that such subsidisation has led not just to artificially low transport resource prices, but also to a mobility pattern of consumption and international production and of work/living, shopping, tourism, etc. which has expanded way beyond what would be socially desirable and taken on the form of becoming 'unsustainable' or, in the words of the environmental economists, 'unchecked'.

Such an unchecked, unsustainable trajectory of world growth appears from this perspective closely associated with the liberalisation of an international trading system based on artificially low transport prices. While it is such trade liberalisation which has been behind a large part of the rapid growth and increased welfare gains in the OECD economies and more recently newly industrializing countries, allowing those economies to realise the increasing returns associated with specialisation, as 'new' trade and later on 'new' growth theory have illustrated, such concentration of activities in particular locations has been based on the assumption that the mobility and transport costs associated with (international) trading were and would remain relatively minimal (as in the case of flowers) or could be, as in the extreme case of 'just-in-time' production, 'cost-shifted' to society at large.

6.5 New sustainable growth and ICT

The fundamental challenge which the emergence of the new information and communication technology paradigm is bringing to the forefront is the shift towards a new growth and development paradigm based less on mobility and specialisation and more on proximity and flexibility. The experience of tele-working shows that ICT certainly cannot ever completely substitute for personal contacts; what it can do is greatly reduce the frequency of journeys to work, meetings, conferences, etc. The challenge is much more than a technological one, it is a much broader societal and economic one. Is indeed mobility, both nationally and internationally, endemic to the concept itself of economic growth and personal interaction and well-being?

We do not believe so. Many of the structural changes described in Chapter 4, such as regional integration or the increased tradability of services, correspond to a new, more proximity- and flexibility-based international trade pattern emerging. It is a pattern in which trade of manufactured goods is becoming governed by the interaction between reaping economies of scale and proximity to consumer markets. Trade in raw materials and commodities is increasingly becoming less 'raw': the materials are transformed near the location of extraction, thus increasing the value added of the shipped transformed commodities: in other words, there becomes a reduction in cross-ocean manufacturing trading in favour of foreign investment. At the same time, trade in services, based as it is on the sheer costless — also from an environmental point of view — transport of communication in oral, written or image form, will increase exponentially, bringing about a new source of growth and development based on what we would call international network externalities. International tourism would shift increasingly towards computer-controlled sailing ships, airships and other transport modes less damaging to the environment.

However, it is essential not to overestimate the speed of change towards a new path of sustainable development and reduction of environmentally damaging emissions from existing transport and energy systems. We have already stressed the slow pace of institutional change and the inertia of existing systems is very great. There are no reliable statistics of tele-commuting but the very limited data available for the United Kingdom suggest that fewer than 10 per cent of firms make use of tele-working and for those it is still only a small proportion of employees who are affected. However, over 20 per cent of firms with more than a thousand employees were reported as using tele-working for some workers and more are considering it.

Just as this book was being completed there were the first signs of a change in the ideological thrust of the UK government which has dominated policy for the past 15 years. The *Sunday Telegraph* (13 March 1994), in a news report headed 'Tories end love affair with the motor car' (Helm and Neale) reported that:

The government is to abandon a large part of its £23 billion roads programme and postpone many other road projects as part of a marked shift away from support for 'the great car economy'
The move which has been largely forced on the Department of Transport by cuts in public spending, will be promoted by Ministers as a departure from the policies of Lady Thatcher — a champion of the roads lobby. It will also be a clear response to Britain's environmental responsibilities agreed since the United Nations Earth Summit in 1992.
The new rules, a copy of which has been obtained by the *Sunday Telegraph* disclose that Whitehall officials believe present road-building policy, geared to ever-increasing demand, is no longer sustainable.

Welcome though such indications may be, the scale of investment in the old type of infrastructure is still enormous and it will inevitably take a long time to switch transport modes both for work and other journeys. Moreover, the ICT paradigm does not yet affect the energy infrastructure, except indirectly by facilitating the reduction of energy inputs in some industrial processes and domestic systems. To move towards a fully sustainable path of development would require not only a dramatic change in transport infrastructure but also in energy infrastructure towards renewable energy sources (solar power, wind power, etc.). This is still some way off. Probably, therefore, it is more realistic to regard the ICT techno-economic paradigm as potentially an important intermediate stage in the transition to an environmentally sustainable economy, to be succeeded by a more comprehensive 'green' techno-economic paradigm (Freeman, 1992) during the course of the next century.

This does not lessen the importance of moving as rapidly as possible towards a new type of infrastructure and in the final chapter we shall discuss briefly what this implies for public investment policies and other types of neo-Keynesian programmes.

Note

[1] For a discussion of the factors affecting the diffusion of ISDN (Integrated Services Digital Network), see David and Steinmüller (1990) and Mansell (1993).

7

POLICIES FOR EMPLOYMENT: in the long run
we are not all dead

7.1 The urgent need for higher levels of employment

In Chapter 3 we have briefly introduced two alternative scenarios for
the future of ICT-based employment. George Gilder foresees almost
unlimited expansion of new computer-networked services, which
would generate huge new demands on the computer industry, the
telecommunications industry, the education system, all kinds of information services and software activities during the first part of the
twenty-first century. John Lippman on the other hand is typical of
many who deride technical determinism and technological optimism
as media hype and foresee either things continuing much as they are
today or a much darker vision. They are right to be sceptical to some
degree as there is always a danger of looking at a new technology
with rose-coloured spectacles, as was the case with electricity and
indeed with Fordist mass production, whether in the United States or
in Soviet Russia.

No one can accurately predict the future; human beings themselves
have the power to realise or to falsify any such predictions. The value
of contemplating alternative futures lies therefore not in the precision
of any particular forecast but rather in the contribution to the debate
on alternative policies which might influence this future. In this final
chapter we attempt such a modest contribution and we do not wish to
belittle the difficulties and the pain of the transition we are discussing.

We start from the assumption that full employment, or at least
substantial reduction of unemployment, is a very important policy

objective for most if not all countries, for the reasons advanced in
Chapter 1. This is of course a value-judgement but we believe that it
is one which is shared by most governments and international
organisations and (which is more important) by almost the whole
population of our countries. They might differ to some degree on
definitions of 'full employment' and we ourselves believe there is
sometimes a case for using the expression 'active society' to convey
what we mean. Full employment is to some degree associated with
the notion of adult male, 16–65 employment, rather than the flexible
pattern of lifetime work opportunities and education, for men and
women, young and old, full-time or part-time, which we have discussed in Chapter 5 and believe should now be feasible. On the other
hand there is a danger that to drop the expression 'full employment'
could imply acceptance of a large amount of *involuntary* part-time
and casual work. Figure 7.1 illustrates the extent to which *involuntary*
part-time work has increased in Canada in recent years and is typical
of a general trend. Whatever the precise terminology, the goal
should be that work or education should be available for all who
seek it, including the numerous discouraged workers and involuntary part-time workers who today do not find full-time employment
opportunities.

This is not simply some woolly-minded, idealistic goal. It is an
aspiration which is firmly grounded both in economics and other
social sciences. For social psychologists the evidence is clear-cut: the
vast majority of human beings need the opportunity for active participation in the work of society as much for non-economic as for
economic reasons. The hidden costs of high unemployment are
much greater than the more easily measurable economic costs. The
economic advantages of high levels of employment and work-force
participation are obvious and accepted by all schools of economists,
even though they may differ to some degree on how far employment
objectives can be reconciled with other policy objectives.

There is, however, a genuine problem of inflationary cost pressures
if demand exceeds the supply of labour for longish periods. We have
argued that this is by no means an urgent *contemporary* problem. But
it could return. This problem of 'wage restraint' gave rise from the
1960s to the 1980s to numerous attempts by Keynesian economists
and the governments whom they advised to devise and implement
'wages policies' to dampen inflationary pressures (or prices and
incomes policies since it is not only a question of wages). None of
these could be said to have been very successful, except in the short
term. From this experience many drew the conclusion that there was

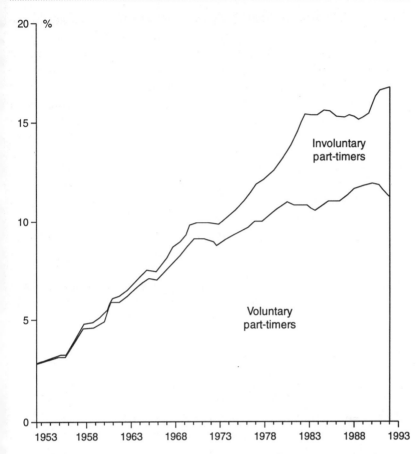

Figure 7.1 Part-time workers as percentage of all employed, Canada, 1953–1992

Source: Statistics Canada, reproduced in Kettle (1994).

indeed a 'natural rate of unemployment' which was unavoidable to counteract inflationary pressures. As we have seen in Chapter 5, the work of Phelps-Brown, Kalecki and Salvati also appears to point in this direction, albeit on a long-term cyclical basis. However, the long-wave theories point to the fact that workers and unions did indeed change their behaviour and show considerable restraint for quite long periods, as in the 1950s, when a low rate of inflation, steady improvements in wages and productivity and a low rate of unemployment went together. The problem is to extend such periods indefinitely into the future.

Fortunately, a number of social trends should facilitate such a change in addition to the pressures exerted by the traumatic experiences of the 1980s and 1990s. There have been huge changes in the industrial and occupational structure of the labour force and especially in Europe there has been a big extension of various forms of work-force consultation and participation. In the last resort it is only a sense of responsibility and social justice, based on direct involvement and sometimes ownership, which can generate a new pattern of behaviour. Constructive social policies can promote big changes in this direction so that endless repetition of an old pattern is by no means inevitable. Social learning is a real phenomenon. The new developments in the world economy and the intensified international competition are also important factors which make a return to inflationary conditions far less likely. For these reasons we would maintain that fears of wage pressures should not be allowed to deflect Europe from the goal of a return to full employment, although avoidance of inflationary spirals must of course remain a consistent goal of monetary policy. It should be noted that ICT goods and services are the one major category where prices have fallen over the last 30 years, often steeply, in defiance of the general inflationary trend. The reduction in costs of chips, computers and telecommunications is truly astonishing (Chapter 3) and itself gives substance to the view that an ICT-based economy could be rather successful in keeping inflation at bay. But could it generate the jobs?

7.2 ICT and future sources of new employment

We certainly are not suggesting that it will be easy for Europe to generate a large number of new jobs. Nor will it be easy to retrain large numbers of people. Many new jobs will still be needed for unskilled or low-skilled people for a long time to come. It is essential to realise that, even if the optimistic scenario discussed in Chapter 3 could be realised, only a minority of the new jobs needed would actually be in the ICT industries and services themselves, or indeed in ICT occupations in other industries and services. On balance we believe, for example, that the fairly optimistic forecasts of the US Bureau of Labour for growth of employment for software engineers and software programmers are much more likely to be realised than the more pessimistic forecasts often heard, both in Europe and the United States. The Japanese Minister for Telecommunications estimated that multi-media services would generate 2.4 million new jobs in Japan by 2010. However, the total number of new *software* jobs generated directly either in Europe or the United States would probably be less than a million. Yet more than twenty million new jobs are needed in Europe in the next decade.

The job creation effects of the scenario outlined in Table 3.2 would not just be felt in software occupations or even mainly in software activities. They would be felt in many other service industries as well as in the manufacture of computers, telecommunication equipment and other electronic products. As we have argued in Chapters 3 and 4, the main effects would not be so much in hardware as in the area of information services, data banks, publishing, education, training and health services. However, there are important complementarities between hardware and software, manufacturing and services, and various types of services. Software professionals can seldom provide the type of interactive services which are needed except in collaboration with experienced professionals in other fields, just as they have to collaborate with engineers and managers in the design of manufacturing systems. Hybrid professionals might very well dominate in the end. 'Multi-media project coordinator' may well be the fastest-growing occupation in the next decade even though it has not yet entered the official classification. This can be seen already in the tendency for informatics to become one of the specialisations for other types of engineer rather than the sole specialisation. Many other skilled and less skilled workers will be needed in other industries and services, stimulated by Keynesian multiplier effects.

However, Lippman is undoubtedly right that a new pattern of consumption cannot be forced on consumers. If his interpretation of the Cerritos experiment is right then there would be little job growth potential in those particular interactive services. But there are several reasons for believing that whatever may have happened in Cerritos it would be wrong to draw overall pessimistic conclusions either about the diffusion of ICT or about the perspectives for job creation in the long term in general.

It is important to re-emphasise the point that ICT affects *all* industries and services, creating new investment opportunities everywhere. The impetus which a new techno-economic paradigm can give to the economic system lies not so much in particular products or services as in the boost it can give to investment and to consumer confidence generally. Whilst it is very hard to predict exactly which products or services will achieve the highest growth rates or when, there can now be no doubt about the pervasive stimulus to the economy from ICT. The extent and duration of this stimulus will however depend on public policies which are adopted over the next few years. So will many other aspects of ICT itself be 'shaped' by social pressures and public policies.

We are now in a position to sum up the main points presented in Chapters 2 to 6 and indicate their policy implications:

(i) Whilst economic theory has pointed to compensation mechanisms generating new employment to replace jobs which are lost through technical change, no one has claimed that this process is instantaneous or painless. Economists differ however on the extent to which they would rely on self-adjusting market-clearing mechanisms or on active public investment and labour market policies (Chapter 2).

(ii) Virtually all economists agree that the world economy has experienced a deep crisis of structural adjustment in the 1980s and early 1990s and hence that various forms of *structural* unemployment have become a very serious problem (Chapter 2).

(iii) In our view, shared by an increasing number of our colleagues, this crisis of structural adjustment has been associated with the diffusion of a set of revolutionary new technologies, which we have designated as information and communication technology (ICT) (Chapter 3).

(iv) These technologies, although they have a vast range of present and future applications, do not yet easily match the inherited previous skill profile, management organisation, industrial structure or institutional framework more generally (Chapter 3).

(v) Countries differ widely in the occupational and sectoral composition of their labour force, in the speed of their structural adjustment, in the flexibility of their work-force organisation and other institutions in their response to new technologies and hence in the relative growth rates of new sectors and of trade (Chapter 4).

(vi) A major new factor in the world economy has been the very rapid 'catch-up' of the Eastern and now increasingly South Asian economies. They have experienced the most rapid structural change, the highest rates of employment growth and the most rapid diffusion of ICT (Chapter 4).

(vii) Strong, but not exclusively related to this Asian success, has been the intensified international competition. This can no longer be disregarded as a source of employment loss in OECD countries, especially for less skilled workers in both manufacturing and services (Chapter 4).

(viii) 'Flexibility' as a response to this intensified competition can take various forms: reduction of wages and social benefits or a further more pronounced structural shift towards high skill and high value-added sectors and activities. The education infra-structure is still largely geared to earlier production systems. Success in the latter strategy involves therefore big changes in education, training, skills, R&D, design and management ('Get smarter or get poorer') (Chapter 5).

(ix) The present transport and communication infrastructure has been developed to handle a vast and still increasing number of cars, trucks and aeroplanes. The overloading of this infrastruc-ture is bumping up against limits of urban congestion and atmospheric pollution (Chapter 6).

(x) ICT has the potential to alleviate some of these problems but the necessary new infrastructure and services are still in the early stages of development (Chapter 6).

These points lead to the following policy conclusions with respect to new employment and employment policies:

(a) To realise the vast future job creation potential of ICT will require substantial further investment in the telecommunication infrastructure ('Information Highways and Byways') and related data banks, services and buildings. We discuss this in Section 7.3.

(b) The transformation of the skill profile will require heavy 'intan-gible' investment in the education and training infrastructure. We discuss this in Section 7.4.

(c) The scale of the unemployment problem and the intensity of low-wage competition, especially in Europe (Section 7.5), makes it necessary to adopt other measures to generate and sustain new employment in the medium and long term. These would aim to foster a 'sheltered' second-tier economy based on non-traded services, construction and environmental improvement. These ideas are discussed in Section 7.6, followed by conclusions in Section 7.7.

7.3 Investment in physical infrastructure

Recovery from recession is the first essential in restoring the process of job creation. Moreover, the recovery has to be strong enough that total output growth *exceeds* the growth rate of labour productivity as in the 1950s and 1960s. Circumstances vary in different countries but in general it can be said that both in Europe and Japan there was a

strong case in 1993–94 for a variety of counter-cyclical Keynesian measures affecting both monetary and fiscal policies. However, in the
short and medium term a new form of Keynesian public investment
policy is likely to prove the most effective. This is in any case essential
to provide the basic infrastructure for an ICT-based economy.

Whilst it is commonly agreed today that information and communication technology (ICT) is indeed a very pervasive and important
technology and most governments, whether in rich or poor countries,
have already adopted some specific policies to support it, when it
comes to investment and specifically to counter-cyclical public and
private investment policies most governments have until recently
been bereft of ideas and imagination. The influence of an old techno-
economic paradigm could still be clearly seen in the measures
announced by various governments in the 1980s and early 1990s con-
centrating mainly on the older industries and infrastructures — road-
building, cars, steel, oil, construction, etc. — and with little to say
about new technologies. Two exceptions were the technology policy
announced in 1993 by the Clinton–Gore administration and the
Delors White Paper. We shall discuss these proposals later in this section. Both of them envisage a significant role for public as well as for
private investment for 'Information Highways' and for 'wiring up'
schools and hospitals.

There is of course nothing wrong with providing a special stimulus
to the traditional construction industry. It was badly needed in
Europe, Japan and many other countries in 1992–94. But such a stimulus provides a wonderful opportunity also to promote the diffusion
and new applications of ICT. Although the 'intelligent building' is
recognised in Japan as extremely important for the 1990s and the
twenty-first century, the concept has been slow to diffuse elsewhere.
Whereas everyone in the United States or Europe will recognise that a
fighter aircraft or a warship or even a machine tool may these days
have an electronic content of 50 per cent or more of its total value,
very few people recognise that major buildings may have an electronic content of 20–30 per cent and that in future they have to be
designed and constructed to accommodate and use this big ICT
investment. The office buildings, banks, hospitals, schools and other
structures used by the service industries may now contain as much or
more hardware and software investment as factories and process
plants. The extensive use of ICT in office buildings actually permits
considerable capital-saving in floor space. IBM offices in both Japan
and the United Kingdom already have achieved economies of 20 per
cent or more through the introduction of 'hot desking' or the 'virtual

office'. Energy savings in temperature control systems are also important and have been shown to save as much as 30 per cent in some
new hospitals.

In his pioneering study of 'intelligent buildings', David Gann (1992)
shows how ICT is transforming not only the design of buildings and
communication systems, but also how this is changing the structure
of the building industry itself in Japan. Keynesian programmes offer
an ideal opportunity to diffuse new technologies and to promote the
necessary collaboration between users, construction firms, and equipment and software suppliers. But there is so far too little sign of any
such coordinated policy initiative. This is only one example of what is
a general problem. Similar considerations apply even more to transport systems. For the reasons discussed in Chapter 6 it is extremely
doubtful whether a simple fiscal stimulus to the automobile industry
and further public investment in road-building programmes are
what is needed in any major industrial country. Indeed it is probably
the opposite of what is needed. For all kinds of reasons the old mass
production and use of automobiles with internal combustion engines
is approaching the limits of traffic congestion, air pollution, environmental degradation, acceptable accident rates and car ownership.
The new ICT offers great possibilities for reducing (not eliminating)
journeys to work, journeys to shop and other types of travel. In combination with public transport systems it also offers great possibilities
for reducing traffic congestion and pollution in urban areas, as well
as providing better public transport facilities for those who are at
present deprived. It is into these areas that imaginative forward-
looking schemes of public investment should be directed.

Both in the case of construction and transport what is needed is
intimate collaboration between the ICT industries, both hardware and
software, and the public and private entrepreneurs in these sectors.
Public investment programmes provide an opportunity for the stimu-
lation of such collaboration in many sectors and for the development
of all kinds of new telecommunication-based data networks and other
networking services, sometimes using 'intelligent buildings'. Linking
up all schools and hospitals to 'information highways' is essential, as
proposed both in the Clinton–Gore proposals and the Delors White
Paper. The 'Highways' (trunk networks) are actually often already in
place: it is the 'Byways', the access roads and 'ramps' and all the
many interconnections which are needed.

In health services, whereas very advanced technologies and instruments including virtual reality (VR) may be used in surgery and (less
frequently) in diagnosis, the computerisation of medical records, of

the treatment of patients, the transmission of relevant information between different parts of the system and advice on preventive medicine and treatment still leaves a lot to be desired. Here too there is enormous scope for imaginative initiatives, which would have multiple effects in many other parts of the economy as well as in the social services and the electronic industries themselves. Early experience suggests that patient-based lifetime medical information systems can both improve the quality and reduce the cost of health care (Pollak, 1985 and 1990).

All these examples demonstrate that neo-Keynesian public investment programmes in the 1990s need a neo-Schumpeterian flavour. The scope and content of such programmes will obviously vary from country to country, depending on industrial structure, specific local priorities, resource endowment and so forth. But the general principle of improving 'structural competitiveness' (Perez, 1990) by stimulating the diffusion of new technology and the growth of 'development blocs' (to use the Swedish term) or 'filières' (to use the French term), based on extensive networking and user–producer links, will apply everywhere. It is a time for social innovations leading to coordination of investment policies, technology policy, industrial policy, training policy and regional policy. There are already examples of the successful use of such policies at the regional level in Asian countries, such as Singapore (Mansell and Jenkins, 1992). For full-scale sustained recovery during the 1990s they will need to be far more widely deployed, as is clearly recognised in the Delors White Paper.

We have noted that many proposals for public investment in the early 1990s still bore the stamp of an old techno-economic paradigm. However, there was already more imaginative emphasis on using public investment and procurement to advance new technology in the United States pronouncements on *technology policy* (Clinton and Gore, 1993). The Clinton–Gore policy statement (February 1993) on 'Technology and Economic Growth' stated boldly:

American technology must move in a new direction to build economic strength and spur economic growth. The traditional federal role in technology development has been limited to support of basic science and mission-oriented research in the Defense Department, NASA, and other agencies. This strategy was appropriate for a previous generation but not for today's profound challenges. We cannot rely on the serendipitous application of defense technology to the private sector. We must aim directly at these new challenges and focus our efforts on the new opportunities before use, recognizing that government can play a key role helping private firms develop and profit from innovations.

The statement then went on to specify in more detail how these bold objectives might be achieved, for example, by:

Redirecting the focus of our national efforts toward technologies crucial to today's businesses and a growing economy, such as information and communication, flexible manufacturing, and environmental technologies

and

Support for a national telecommunications infrastructure and other information infrastructures critical for economic expansion.

These new policies will be implemented through major changes in the Federal Government structure itself, in which

The new National Economic Council will monitor the implementation of new policies and provide a forum for coordinating technology policy with the policies of the tax, trade, regulatory, economic development, and other economic sectors.

Throughout, the statement placed very great emphasis on ICT infrastructure and under a heading entitled 'Information Superhighways' it stated:

Efficient access to information is becoming critical for all parts of the American economy. Banks, insurance companies, manufacturing concerns, and many other business operations now depend on high-speed communication links. Many more businesses can take advantage of such systems if they are reliable, easy to use, and inexpensive. Such systems would also be of enormous value to schools, hospitals, and other public organizations. Even the most remote school could be connected to state-of-the-art information.
Hospitals could call in experts for consultation even if the expert is far from the patient. Accelerating the introduction of an efficient, high-speed communication system can have the same effect on US economic and social development as public investment in the railroads had in the 19th century. It would provide a critical tool around which many new business opportunities can develop.

This was followed by five more detailed project proposals on ICT, especially policies for the dissemination of new technology and promotion of SME. Of particular interest are the proposals for 'Manufacturing Extension Centers' modelled on the Agricultural Extension Service.

The extraordinary productivity gains in American farming throughout this century owe a great deal to the close links between individual farmers and county extension agents.

American manufacturing also needs an effective system. New manufacturing technologies and approaches are available that can lead to dramatic improvements in product quality, cost, and time-to-market. But relatively few US businesses have taken advantage of these new technologies and best practices. The problem is particularly acute among the 360,000 small and medium-sized manufacturers, many of whom are still using 1950s technology.

Workers should play a significant role in the use and spread of manufacturing technology. Workplace experience makes clear that new technologies are implemented most effectively when the knowledge and concerns of workers are included in the process.

To enhance the use of and access to technology, we will:

Create a national network of manufacturing extension centers. Existing state and federal manufacturing extension centers managed through the Department of Commerce provide assistance to a small number of business, but service must be greatly expanded to give all businesses access to the technologies, testing facilities, and training programs they need. Federal funds (to be matched by state and local governments) will support and build on existing state, local, and university programs, with the goal of creating a nation-wide network of extension centers.

It remains to be seen how far these ambitious policy proposals will actually be carried into effect with all the various constraints in the US budgetary and political system. Nevertheless, the proposed policy package was in itself a very significant event, marking as it did the recognition, at the highest level in the most powerful OECD country, of the importance of ICT infrastructure, and of information technology policy issues and indicating constructive and imaginative thinking about these problems. For this reason it has been quoted at some length.

Already there are some big developments with the introduction of the Communication Act in 1994 but inevitably there are both technical and social problems to resolve in designing and constructing the 'Data Highways' and there are different, sometimes conflicting interest groups involved. However, the United States is generally ahead of Europe and Japan in these developments and the US computer journal *Byte* in its issue of March 1994 summed up the key requirements:

To meet the needs of society, the data highway has to be ubiquitous, affordable, easy to use, secure, multi-purpose, information-rich and open. If it's to be economically viable, service providers have to be able to bill customers for the time they spend on the network or the data they use. (p. 48)

To achieve these objectives will mean that the existing precursors of the fully developed system must *all* be linked:

The data highway's backbone will use every wide-area communication technology now known, including fiber, satellites and micro-waves and the on and off ramps connecting users to the backbone will be fiber, coaxial cable, copper and wireless. Data servers will be super-computers, mainframes, minicomputers, micro-computers and massively parallel machines, while a great diversity of clients will populate the end points of the network: conventional PCs, palm-tops and PDAs, smart phones, set-top boxes and TVs. Software used in the network will include operating systems, networking protocols and services, user interfaces, data bases, data sources (or content) and a new generation of smart *middleware* (e.g. General Magic's agent-based Telescript) that will help users navigate the network. (p. 48)

As in the earlier case of electricity, some of the most important innovations will be interface innovations (such as 'Middleware') enabling different systems to interconnect. Paul David has described these innovations as 'Gateway Innovations' and demonstrated their crucial role in network evolution, as well as their significance for public policy in relation to standards (David and Bunn, 1988). Government has a major role to play in support of R&D, in encouraging innovations, in ensuring universal access, in subsidising certain categories of users and in resolving key regulatory issues.

All of these are also major issues in the development of the European ICT infrastructure. For more than a decade the EU has attempted to strengthen European capability and European cooperation through programmes such as ESPRIT, RACE and IMPACT.

Although not quite so ambitious in their plans as the Clinton–Gore proposals, the EU and various EU member governments have recently begun to put more stress on proposals to link up users with the new ICT infrastructure. These are very varied in different member countries as might be expected in view of the variety of circumstances and much will depend on national and regional initiatives. The Delors Report (CEC, 1993) shows great awareness of the role of ICT in job creation and employment policies. It proposes an 'Action Plan' based on five priorities (p. 23) to strengthen four key applications of ICT in Europe (Tables 7.1 and 7.2).

To promote these objectives it proposed an investment in EU Telecommunications of 67 billion ECU (p. 27) from 1994 to 1999, with, however, only a small contribution from the EU budget itself (p. 26). From this it is evident (as well as from the rest of the Report) that the CEC has for some time been well aware of the role of the telecommu-

Table 7.1 The Delors Report's 'Action Plan': ICT in Europe

Priority	Means
1. Promote the use of information technologies	— launch European projects on applications and public services (transport, health, training, education and civil protection) and strengthen cooperation between administrations (IDA programme): — promote teleworking — ensure closer involvement of users in the drafting and implementation of technology policies
2. Provide basic trans-European services	— develop the basic networks (ISDN and broadband) — ensure network interoperability — ensure closer coordination between telecommunications policies and aid from the Structural Funds
3. Continue to create an appropriate regulatory framework	— end distortions of competition — guarantee a universal service — speed up standardisation — protect privacy and ensure the security of information and communication systems — extend intellectual property law liberalisation and harmonisation
4. Develop training on new technologies	— encourage acquisition of the basic knowledge required in order to use new technologies and exploit their potential — ensure widespread use of new technologies in teaching and training — adapt the training for engineers and researchers
5. Improve industrial and technological performance	— increase the RTD effort and adapt it to the new market conditions (fourth framework programme) — promote industry and technology watch — take up the results of RTD in industrial applications — negotiate equitable conditions of access to the competitive market at world level

Source: CEC (1993).

Table 7.2 The Delors Report's 'Action Plan': promotion of four priority applications

Teleworking, teletraining, telemedicine and links between administrations	
Teleworking —	Projects are already under way in the Member States. The Community would support pilot programmes on the establishment of a trans-frontier network for the management of human resources
Teletraining —	The objective is to establish a network linking over 100 universities or colleges by 1996 and giving them all access to common training modules
Telemedicine —	By the year 2000 multimedia links are to be established between the main cancer research centres, bone marrow banks and social security centres
Links between administrations—	To improve the operation of the internal market (taxation, customs, statistics), it is essential to facilitate the interchange of data between administrations and to provide companies and the public with easier access to this information.

Source: CEC (1993).

nication infrastructure in improving the competitiveness of the EU and promoting job regeneration but at the same time is counting mainly on national schemes funded by private investors, with the emphasis still mainly on the trans-European highways rather than local and regional networks. Europe still has a long way to go before it has the ICT infrastructure necessary for structural competitiveness in the twenty-first century.

Many economists might well agree with most or all of the proposals in the Clinton–Gore package or the Delors package. They are after all mostly concerned with areas of 'market failure' and infrastructure which have traditionally been accepted as the legitimate concern of public policies and initiatives. With the advent of 'new' growth theory (Romer, 1986, 1990; Lucas, 1988) there is now also a renewed and much more generally accepted converging view that another of the most critical factors behind economic growth and development is, and has been, educational investment.

Education is increasingly seen as an *essential* investment in learning capacity and societal communication, increasing in the first instance the overall knowledge base of society, rather than the individual's 'human capital'. The 'social rate of return' is higher than the 'individual rate of return'. From this perspective, too, the inherent contradiction in education is one between a broadening of the knowledge base with the aim of keeping learning options open as long as possible and specialisation with the acquisition of particular technical skills. While the latter are generally speaking an integral part of professional or occupational 'skills', their introduction in education requires a much closer interaction with the labour market. Without this, the acquisition of such technical specialized skills can sometimes amount to investment in 'evaporating wealth'. Generalised learning information and communication skills have a more enduring value, enabling individuals to adapt to changing patterns of demand.

7.4 Education as a form of social infrastructural investment

Very many parents and grandparents must have watched with admiration and amazement as their children and grandchildren learned to excel in computer games, which they themselves could hardly tackle. Not only do many children concentrate for hours on end on games such as 'Mario is missing' or 'Sonic the Hedgehog' but they will go on day after day even though the obsolescence rate in these games is high and fashion plays a big part. Yet the very same children will often say 'School is boring' or 'Homework is boring' or 'Maths is boring' or 'Geography is boring'. Here surely is a tremendous challenge for the entire education profession all over the world. Learning should be exciting and interesting, not boring, and often it should be fun.

Some ICT enthusiasts are so impressed by the versatility and potential of ICT that they imagine that the regular educational institutions can be partly, or even completely bypassed. Some commercial interests also see great possibilities in developing the 'home' market for education while some educationists are so depressed by conditions in schools and what are seen as the contemporary failures of the system that they also flirt with the idea of 'deschooling' to a greater or lesser extent. Finally, there are people who see this as an opportunity to reduce public expenditure.

It is true that there is a greatly increased potential for people of all ages (certainly not only children) to learn all kinds of things at home and it is certainly desirable to exploit this potential in a variety of ways. However, in our view the idea of displacing the formal education system is both wrong and dangerous. Certainly the schools and universities can be greatly improved, can be more exciting, and can

make far greater use of ICT than they do today but they are needed
more than ever for the following reasons.

(1) Although children can indeed show great concentration and
determination in playing computer games and some can learn a
lot at home, there are also subjects and activities which can less
easily be learnt at home or not at all. Most children benefit from
interacting with other children and learn from each other, as well
as from media and from teachers. Most also need some personal
help, care and guidance in their studies. Computer games, CD-
ROM and multi-media services cannot entirely displace teachers
any more than books can.

(2) Schools are extremely important for socialisation and communication. As we have seen, one of the major needs of the future work-
place is communication skills. It is difficult, if not impossible to
acquire these in isolation or purely through ICT. Not only in work
but also in social and political life, communication and socialisation are extremely important. Schools have a major role in social
cohesion and in national culture.

(3) The home environment for many children does not facilitate
home learning on any kind of regular or systematic basis. One
consequence of deschooling would be to divide the population
into information-rich households and information-poor households. Whilst this would not correspond exactly to income
distribution, it would generally further handicap the children of
less wealthy parents, who are already disadvantaged education-
ally in various ways. One of the major advantages of the school
system is universality, providing children from all kinds of
households with opportunities to learn. Whilst it is true that
there are also some children who do not learn in the formal
system but do learn through other channels, there would almost
certainly be a massive decline in educational standards of a large
number of children if deschooling was pushed a long way.

(4) In addition to the *social* and *educational* reasons for improving
rather than bypassing the formal eduction system, there are also
strong *economic* reasons. Much equipment which cannot conceiv-
ably be provided to every single household can be provided at
reasonable cost in educational institutions. Libraries are an
obvious case and the argument applies *a fortiori* to CD-ROM
libraries, video libraries, and other ICT resources and equipment,
especially virtual reality equipment (VR). But the argument also
applies to laboratories, art rooms, workshops, sports facilities,
music rooms, theatres, and much else. It is true that many profes-

sional people today may have their own libraries, including video libraries and their own workshops. It is also true that there is a tendency as incomes grow to prefer ownership to borrowing but the same people who own many books usually also make use of libraries and other collective facilities. The children of deprived households have no chance if they do not have access to public facilities. There are many indivisibilities in education as in industry and commerce and education can no more be a purely individualistic activity than production. 'Video-on-demand' (VOD) is the goal of some of the big consortia which are being formed to deliver information services and entertainment to households via Cable TV networks or satellite but even if they succeed, as they probably will, this will not be a cheap service, so that there will still be big economic advantages in providing education services through the education system.

(5) Finally, schools do not only have an educational and a socialisation function, they also have what some people call a 'custodial' function. Even if a larger number of parents work at home they do need time to work relatively free of interruptions. Children also need time to *learn* free of interruptions from parents, brothers, sisters, friends, etc. Indeed, a very strong argument can be made that far from children spending *less* time at school, they should spend *more*.

Organisations such as Education Extra have been formed precisely in order to promote and extend *after*-school but *at*-school activities. Such activities have many advantages:

(a) They enable the community to take advantage of the public investment in buildings and other facilities, which otherwise is idle most of the time.

(b) They enable children to broaden their learning to a wider range of subjects, activities, societies, etc. Many of them greatly improve their communication skills, other social skills and ICT capability.

(c) They enable children to do their homework at school. This is exceptionally important for disadvantaged children with difficult home conditions but more and more schools are finding that it improves the quality of after-school learning for many pupils who find it harder to work once they get home.

(d) They enable schools to become a focus for community life more generally. They can involve local industry and commerce, who find it much easier to interact with the school in these after-school activities and indeed to promote some of them.

(e) Many schools already have a wide range of activities including 'self-supported studies' and 'industry-supported studies' in what are technically after-school hours. They are often the focus of computer-based activities too. Indeed, both schools and universities would become the focus of all kinds of ICT-based activities for local communities.

(f) The extension of these activities together with increased provision of nursery school education would greatly improve the possibilities for women, as well as men to work more flexible hours. They would also provide new opportunities for adult education, as already indicated in the case of the Motorola experiment (Wiggenhorn, 1990).

Therefore we would argue the very reverse of the deschooling argument in favour of an enhanced role for the public education system in disseminating and using ICT-based media of all kinds. In fact we would go much further and argue that it is essential for public education policy to play an active role in developing new course material in cooperation with industry. To develop new modules for new courses in every discipline and combination of disciplines and to keep them up to date is an absolutely enormous educational undertaking. It requires the active participation of the teaching profession at all levels and not just in a few specialised 'technology' schools.

At this point in the argument the objection is often raised: the schools and the teachers are too conservative or even that they are Luddites. It is indeed true that the teaching profession or parts of it have not always been specially receptive to new technologies. But just as in the case of industry and commerce, where there is also often resistance to the introduction of ICT, it is essential to understand the reasons for this suspicion or hostility. It is also essential to study the experience of successful institutional and technical change to understand why it often fails, whether in the classroom, the boardroom, the factory, or the bank.

The commonest cause of failure in industrial innovation is failure to involve the *users* of a new process or product in its design, development and application. Numerous case studies over the past 30 years support this generalisation (e.g. Rothwell *et. al.* 1974; Freeman, 1982). There is no reason to suppose that education is any different in this respect. Lack of user-friendliness was the biggest problem with computer software and computer-based innovations generally for a long time. Consequently it is not at all surprising that teachers, like many other people, were put off in the 1960s and 1970s by the early attempts to woo them with educational technology. They had the strong impression that they were being pressurised by people who had little knowledge of classroom activities, of education itself and of the specific disciplines they were teaching, and being asked to use material that neither they nor their pupils found particularly helpful. Not surprisingly, then, early efforts often failed as did similar early efforts with robotics and office computers. Most of the teachers knew little or nothing about ICT which did not help matters either.

Now the situation has changed dramatically. Not only the teachers but the children are the users of ICT in education. The children are now often happy with computers. In Britain and in many other countries public policies have helped to achieve widespread availability of PCs in schools and even to achieve very early, small-scale applications of VR and CD-ROM. Much of the software is easy to use and as we have argued computer games are so popular that they have familiarised a new generation with interactive learning. Many more of the teachers are now also computer-numerate. Finally, the technology and software have improved so much, costs have come down so low and quality has improved so much that the band-wagon is now rolling along fast.

However, every new ICT product has to be developed with care and attention to user needs. Whether we are talking about the case of virtual reality (VR) software for medical students or aircraft pilots, and soon for many other education and training applications, or remedial mathematics CD-ROM for children with maths phobia, the rule is the same: user-friendliness is an absolutely essential ingredient. The computer companies learnt this the hard way as the market expanded from the first patient and mathematically inclined professional scientists to the wider market in industry and goverment. Now the lesson has often to be relearnt with every new educational software package that is produced. The very long gestation period of VR also illustrates this point (Sherman and Judkins, 1992).

It is quite possible that once information highways, byways and networks are established a higher proportion of teaching and learning will be on the basis of networked services and CD-ROMs, etc. will be rather less important but the same considerations apply in developing networked educational services or VR techniques.

Consequently, a policy for developing the use of ICT in education should be based on the following principles:

(i) Every multi-media team to develop a CD-ROM, CD-I, VR or other IT-based product for education or even for 'edu-tainment' should include not only a software professional but also an educational professional. Public education policy should aim to provide all teachers with sabbaticals during which they should be attached to public or private agencies which are designing and developing the thousands of new titles which are needed. They would join a multi-media team or VR team working in their own subject area. Such a team might typically comprise: (1) a multi-media project coordinator (a job title not yet in the occupational classification but which will become commonplace in the next century); (2) a computer software professional; (3) a teacher on sabbatical leave; (4) an artist or film or TV script writer or designer with experience in graphics and animation; (5) a good *humanities generalist;* (6) a researcher in the relevant field with strong communication skills. They would typically work for 6–12 months as a team and would of course interact with relevant pupils, play-groups, students or whatever.

(ii) The education system should stimulate and assist the formation of some multi-media teams and VR teams in both the private and the public sector, partly through the secondment of teachers, partly through the use of educational activities for trial development and partly through such organisations as the British Centre for Education Technology (CET) and the Open University (OU) and their equivalent in other countries. Just as the wartime radar development required cooperation of industry, government and universities, so too does this vast educational R&D activity. It needs to be promoted by a lead institution (in the British case probably CET) which is itself involved in the design and development of new products, but is also a network coordinator and sponsor of many other projects.

(iii) Constant up-dating of ICT products is necessary and it is especially important to achieve flexible adaptation to local needs. This again points to the need to involve schools and teachers. In Europe the multi-cultural context and the experience of cultural diversity with CD-I and similar products from other firms create a specially favourable context.

Some people would still argue that the existing education and training systems in Europe appear to be 'stuck' with a completely outdated 'production function' at least one to two hundred years old. Education sometimes seems to be the only sector in the economy which appears to have remained immune from the technological and information revolution which has taken place over the last thirty years, yet education is precisely that activity which could thrive with new technology, in which the possibilities to improve the efficiency in transferring knowledge and generating learning capacity are practically unlimited.

From an organisational perspective, too, education could cynically be described as the last bastion of Departmentalism and Taylorism, totally unsuited to respond to the challenge of interdisciplinary and adult and permanent education, but rather geared towards other custodial social functions such as keeping youngsters off the street, etc. For many it is difficult to see how such a medieval system would be able to adjust to the new challenges of a more lifelong interdisciplinary learning system. Education appears from this perspective as an infrastructural investment of very low efficiency which is in urgent need of being revitalised, given its crucial importance for future (employment) growth and competitiveness. Yet the more developed OECD countries have more resources to devote to education on smaller youth cohorts than most of the developing and industrialising countries, some of which appear to be creating more dynamic, more work integrated education and training systems making full use of the new information and communication technologies. Developed countries, and in particular the European countries with their older, probably most 'rusted' educational systems should look urgently at their existing education and training systems with the aim of improving the transition process from school to work, creating those conditions (including financial and work organisation conditions) which will generate both the demand for and supply of flexible life-time-based learning, and provide more appropriate basic education for the least educated. Success in future international competition will depend very much on the effectiveness of this form of education infrastructural investment and the determination to enlist the full cooperation of the teaching profession in these changes and raise their professional status to reflect their true importance to society. The traditional function of education in sustaining and transmitting national culture should of course never be lost sight of; it could even be revitalised by these new approaches.

7.5 International trade competition and future employment

Despite the problems discussed in Chapter 4, we believe that Western Europe can remain competitive in world trade even with a rising level of living standards and environmental standards, provided appropriate policies are adopted for structural competitiveness.

First of all, there is the obvious lesson of historical experience. The expansion of the world economy over the past two hundred years has been accompanied by the increased participation of many formerly poor and backward countries in world trade. Some of them were able to catch up or even surpass the wealthier countries in export performance. Yet this did not prevent countries such as Britain, Netherlands or France from continuing to raise their living standards and enjoy prosperity. Indeed the growth of world trade provided their industries with expanding markets as well as increased competition in their home markets. Those who fear international trade competition often forget this two-edged nature of international trade. A prosperous China, a prosperous India, a prosperous Russia and a prosperous Brazil would certainly present enormous and intense competition for Western Europe; they would also present enormous opportunities for West European exports. Moreover, the example of South Korea already shows that catch-up can be a process which leads to better conditions of labour, as well as higher wages.

Of course, this trade needs to be conducted fairly under agreed rules of international cooperation and regulation and it will not be easy to handle all the disputed issues which may arise. There may well be a case for protecting particular industries for varying periods in some countries but less in Europe than in poorer countries, as is indeed recognised in trade agreements. There will also be an increasing need to take into account international transport costs for environmental reasons discussed in Chapter 6. Many industrial sectors of existing comparative advantage in the OECD countries appear crucially dependent on low or even subsidised energy costs. Countries concerned about the environmental degradation caused by such industries fear the loss of international competitiveness in such sectors and are only prepared to tackle the environmental problems associated with such sectors in an internationally coordinated way. There is thus a strong case for wider international efforts to regulate social as well as environmental standards in world trade competition. The ILO and the UN environmental organisations have an increasingly important role to play in the family of international organisations.

There is here, however, the danger of a certain stalemate developing. Free trade in the absolute sense, as within the framework of an economic integration process like the EU, has a powerful reallocation and deregulation impact. It brings to the forefront in an abrupt and relatively immediate way the consumer costs associated with various trade barriers and national regulations. This deregulation impact is to some extent absolute, explaining partially why the initial trade-enhancing impact of economic integration is generally described as 'negative integration' (Balassa, 1961) and the easiest to achieve. 'Positive integration' involves the setting up of common rules and regulations and is in general far more difficult to achieve. The present debates in Europe about economic union and the failure to come up in the Maastricht Treaty with a common social chapter, let alone agreements on a new common energy or other environmental taxes, illustrate quite clearly the major difficulties in arriving at such positive integration.

From this perspective, individual 'beggar-thy-neighbour' responses to unemployment, often under the pretence of free trade, are particularly disturbing. Such policy responses represent to some extent the mirror image of the traditional protectionist response. They include various attempts at reducing domestic labour costs relative to major competitors, through reductions in or even abolition of minimum social legislation, environmental rules and regulations, etc. Free trade in this social deregulation sense has undoubtedly a negative connotation. The benefits of trade should lead to better international allocation of resources, thus increasing welfare at the world level. The response of the developed countries should not be to try to adjust downwards, to reduce social achievements so as to remain competitive in sectors in which they *de facto* no longer can achieve comparative advantage. Such negative adjustment trends contrast sharply with the positive adjustment policy proposals made since the mid-1980s by organisations such as the OECD and aimed at helping workers, firms and sectors to adjust towards higher skills, higher value-added and higher income levels. Developed countries must keep running to stay in the same place.

The impression of a much more competitive international environment is undoubtedly a reflection of the fact that the process of catching up taking place in countries like South and East Asia has been and continues to be successful. This is to be welcomed and a major objective of international policy should be to enable African, Latin American and East European countries also to catch up. The rich developed OECD economies no longer operate in an industrial vacuum where more than 80 per cent of world production or world trade originated from within these countries. The world economy, particularly in the Asian Pacific area, and by and large outside the OECD, has grown and is likely to continue to grow much more rapidly than the old North Atlantic US–European core base. The fact that most of the employment concerns are being voiced in Europe is, from this perspective, not surprising. It is, whether one likes it or not, part of a more general structural shift in the growth and employment pole from Europe–USA to Asia. Europe needs to respond to this not by deregulating its social achievements so as to stay competitive or keep international firms located in Europe, but by investing more in education, training and its own technological and physical infrastructure.

We have argued that, given appropriate policies for infrastructural investment and for structural competitiveness, Europe will be able to compete in international trade in the twenty-first century. However, the very existence of cheap world-wide telecommunication networks will greatly increase the international tradability of services and, given the low environmental cost of such transport of 'ideas' and immaterial 'data', this will tend to shrink the scope of employment in hitherto untradable service sectors (Section 4.7). Furthermore, even though many industries and services in Europe will be able to remain competitive, they may do so only with a reduced labour force. We therefore believe that to secure and sustain a return to full employment conditions it will be necessary to take some active steps to enlarge and encourage the non-tradable 'second tier' of the economy. Otherwise it may become not only an area of shrinking employment but also of Mafia-type activities, flourishing in a semi-legal 'black economy' and using sweated labour, as is only too evident today both in Eastern Europe and many Third World countries.

7.6 A two-tier economy and the 'sheltered' non-tradable sector

There is a need for a further stimulus to employment which would be less vulnerable to the shocks of international competition and the vagaries of the business cycle. In the past such a 'sheltered' sector existed in many countries in public and private service industries. In particular in Japan, for example, the retail trade sector performed this function. With the growing pressures on some service industries to be internationally competitive (Chapter 4) and the efforts to reduce central government expenditures, it has become essential to reconsider the role of the non-traded sector of the economy specifically with respect to employment.

Rosted (1993) and other Danish economists (Jensen and Kjeldsen-Kragh, 1994) have pointed to the great potential for employment growth in personal services often provided at the moment by a combination of the 'black economy' (e.g. in cleaning and repair work) and

DIY activities. They propose changes in the tax system which would facilitate the re-entry of these services from the 'black' and DIY to the normal economy and their subsequent future growth. It is notable that the growth in some of these occupations has been and is projected to be very high indeed (home-health aides, domestic work, etc.) in the United States. The ageing of the population in OECD countries is another important reason for the growth of these services. The fastest-growing occupations in the US Department of Labour estimates from Table 3.4 have been rearranged by ranking them by rate of growth in Table 7.3 and it is very striking that almost all of the very fast growth can be found in four categories:

(1) ICT occupations
(2) Education
(3) Caring personal services
(4) Repair and maintenance

Tax arrangements vary in different countries and there is also variation between central, regional and local government finance, but in many cases the decision to avoid VAT (and the ease of doing so) leads to many of the third and fourth categories being performed largely in the 'black' informal economy. For this reason the Danish proposals

Table 7.3 Occupational employment forecasts, United States, 1990–2005 (% increase)

Home-health aides	+91.7
Systems Analysts & Computer Scientists	+78.9
Computer Programmers	+56.1
Child-care workers	+48.8
Information clerks	+46.9
Registered nurses	+44.4
Nursing aides	+43.4
Cooks	+41.8
Gardeners	+39.8
Lawyers	+35.1
Accountants	+34.5
Secondary schoolteachers	+34.2
Educational assistants	+34.4
Food counter	+34.2
Guards	+33.7
Food preparation	+31.6

Source: US Bureau of Labor Statistics (1992).

for VAT exemption and other tax changes appear eminently sensible. They would also lead to more accurate statistics of employment and unemployment and to the entry of new firms into the area of personal services. Considerable ingenuity will be needed in tax reform but the general objective is clear. The decentralised local government role is very important and there is ample scope for the expansion of local government personal services for the aged, the sick and the needy. Local authorities are far better able to organise and supervise these services than central government but in some countries centralisation of finance and political power does not permit them to do so. There is a need for 'reinventing government' so as to strengthen decentralised institutions, public enterprise and voluntary services as well as market-based services.

Just as the whole area of personal services is in need of rejuvenation and reform, so too is the environmental sphere. The investments required in waste and water management, in emissions control equipment, in alternative low emission transport systems and in recyclable material are substantial in practically all countries. In densely populated areas such as the Netherlands, it is, for example, estimated that the total cost of waste land removal is about $50 bn. The search for alternatives in this case, for example, biological treatment technologies, is as much driven by the need to reduce the accumulated environmental costs of the past as by future promises of huge new market opportunities both domestically and internationally. Many of these environmental needs will require local investments and are likely at least in the short run to generate new employment opportunities. The clean-up of industrial dereliction caused by earlier phases of industrialisation is already an important source of employment in some localities but of course it will usually be accompanied by environmental improvement, including new parks, nature reserves and leisure facilities as well as new public infrastructure. Continuous environmental improvement and personal services could thus constitute the twin supporting pillars of a sheltered economy offering a wide variety of new employment opportunities, related to local needs and circumstances.

7.7 Conclusions

We have argued that a return to full employment is a difficult but by no means impossible task. It requires an imaginative combination of

public and private investment. In the private sector, there is already a
Schumpeterian band-wagon rolling. In spite of the Cerritos experi-
ment there clearly is a strong interest in numerous companies in
Europe and the United States in making large investments in new
ICT-related services based on computer networks, film studios, publishing and both wired and wireless telecommunications. The biggest
mergers and take-over bids in the history of capitalism in the United
States are one indicator of the strategic positioning which is going on.
Moreover, there was already a very high rate of growth in this area in
1992–94 in spite of the recession. This does not mean of course that
everyone involved will be successful. Some ventures will succeed and
some will fail; this is the very nature of the market selection process.

As nother reason for rejecting a highly pessimistic scenario relates to
the *actual* changes in the broad pattern of consumer demand which
are already evident over 50 years or more, whether in Europe, the
United States or Japan. There are three broad areas of long-term
expansion in consumer demand which still have enormous growth
potential. These are (1) education and training, (2) health services and
(3) leisure services, personal services and entertainment, including
catering. The huge growth in demand for the first two services is
often obscured because, in Europe especially, they have mainly been
provided as public services rather than through the market.
Nevertheless, these services together now account for more than 20
per cent of total GDP in both Europe and the United States compared
with little more than 5 per cent in 1938. Expenditure on education
and training alone is now between 5 and 10 per cent of total GDP in
most industrial countries (Table 7.4). Private expenditure on education has been growing rapidly but by far the biggest share is the
public education system. Health accounts in most OECD countries for
a similar fraction of GDP.

As we have already emphasised, it is notable that the BLS forecasts
for future employment growth in the United States from 1990 to 2005
(Table 3.4 and 7.3) show health-related occupations (nurses, nursing
aides, etc.), personal services, education-related occupations, information occupations and catering occupations (chefs, food preparation,
etc.) all among the fastest-growing categories together with software
programmers and systems designers. Together they account for over
half of all the high growth employment which is projected. What is
interesting about these forecasts is not so much the particular occupations as the broad areas of demand growth which they indicate. There
is little doubt that these broad categories of consumer demand will
continue to grow at a high rate over the next decade in Europe and

Table 7.4 Public and private expenditure on education as a
percentage of GDP, 1991

Country	Percentage of GDP
Netherlands	5.8
Canada	7.4
Denmark	6.1
Germany	5.4
Finland	6.6
France	6.0
Ireland	5.9
Japan	5.0
Spain	5.6
United States	7.0
Sweden	6.5

Source: OECD (1992).

Japan as well as the United States.

When we come to consider the actual methods of provision of these services and the employment which may be generated, then again there are some grounds for cautious optimism. To satisfy future demand in these areas will certainly require a lot of labour-intensive activity. Much health care, personal service, child care and education depends completely on personal involvement – the personal caring is the essence of what is being provided. The same is probably true of many leisure, catering and entertainment services including chefs, tour guides, etc. However, although many new opportunities for employment will arise in the personal caring services, this does not mean that there will be no scope for ICT. On the contrary, there are already abundant applications of ICT in health care, in education and training and even in hotels, catering and other leisure activities. Auliana Poon's (1993) thorough study *Tourism, Technology and Competitive Strategies* shows already the profound influence of ICT in reshaping the world-wide tourist industry.

As we have tried to show in Section 7.4, the scope for ICT in home education as well as in laboratory and classroom education is almost infinite. This does not mean that teachers will be displaced. They will be needed more than ever because personal caring attention and skilled management of ICT resources are essential to most educational processes, as well as to health services. What ICT can do is to free teachers to give this personal attention to their pupils and to relieve them of much boring routine repetition of information which can be assimilated far more quickly and reliably by computer edu-tainment, or other interactive educational ICT-based services. The good results achieved in many Asian schools depend on *more* personal teacher–pupil contact than is customary elsewhere, not less.

Nightmare scenarios of total dehumanising computerisation are therefore often misconceived although the humanisation of work remains an extremely important social objective. ICT-based services will not (indeed cannot) replace personal caring services, including most health and education. What they can do is to improve and enhance these services and in some cases to make them more acces-sible to people who otherwise could not enjoy them. Secondly, therefore, the growth in demand for education, health and many other personal caring services can indeed generate also a great increase in employment, including professional ICT-related employ-ment, as well as educationists and health professionals who are also skilled in ICT.

These expanding services can of course vary greatly in quality and in the skill with which they use ICT. The response from consumers will depend very much on these factors. Clearly there is an extremely important role for public policy in setting and achieving high stan-dards in health and education. There is also a major role for public policy in stimulating research, development and demonstration. The combination of jobs that are created may consist of a high proportion of low-pay and low-quality jobs or a high proportion of high value-added and higher-quality jobs. Table 7.5 shows the huge variation in remuneration (compare, for example, SIC 737 with SIC 58) with respect to hourly earnings in these various occupations in the United States. Although these variations are not so great in Europe because of minimum wage legislation and other social provisions, the position is similar in broad outline.

Advocates of reduction in wages and social provisions for unskilled workers in Europe believe that this is necessary to generate employ-ment more quickly, as they believe has already occurred in the United States. However, as the OECD (1993) Interim Report points out, there is a danger of being caught up in a low-wage trap on a long-term basis. To avoid this danger of a permanent large low-wage, low-skill underclass it is essential to press forward with policies for training and high-quality services, so that higher-skill jobs become a steadily

Table 7.5 Non-farm employment and earnings in the United States: selected non-farm industries – number of employees and number and earnings of production workers: 1980 and 1990

1987 SIC[1] code	Industry	All employees Total (1,000)		Production workers			
				Total (1,000)		Average Hourly earnings ($US)	
		1980	1990	1980	1990	1980	1990
41	Local and interurban passenger transit	265	343	244	313	6.34	9.19
42	Trucking and warehousing	1,280	1,638	1,121	1,427	9.13	11.72
481	Telephone communication	1,072	910	779	654	8.72	14.14
483	Radio and television broadcasting	192	236	154	195	7.44	12.72
49	Electric, gas and sanitary services[3]	829	961	678	762	8.90	15.24
491	Electric services	391	457	316	353	9.12	15.82
(F)	Wholesale trade	5,292	6,205	4,328	4,985	6.95	10.79
(G)	Retail trade[3]	15,018	19,683	13,484	17,434	4.88	6.76
58	Eating and drinking places	4,626	6,565	4,256	5,957	3.69	4.97
63	Insurance carriers	1,224	1,453	854	976	6.29	11.19
701	Hotels and motels	1,038	1,595	954	1,413	4.45	6.99
723	Beauty shops	284	373	264	334	4.26	7.10
731	Advertising	153	238	116	171	8.07	13.52
737	Computer and data processing services	304	784	254	612	7.16	15.10
753	Automotive repair shops	350	533	297	437	6.52	9.67
80	Health services[3]	5,278	7,844	4,712	6,974	5.68	10.41
805	Nursing and personal care facilities	997	1,420	898	1,283	4.17	7.25
806	Hospitals	2,750	3,547	2,522	3,247	6.06	11.79
81	Legal services	498	919	427	758	7.35	14.21

[1] 1987 Standard Industrial Classification.
[2] Excludes government.
[3] Includes industries not shown separately.
Source: US Bureau of Labor Statistics, Bulletin 2370, supplement to *Employment and Earnings*, July 1991; and *Employment and Earnings*, monthly, March 1992.

higher proportion of the total. The diffusion of ICT can contribute a great deal to this process. However, it must be recognised that a wide spectrum of high-, medium- and low-skill jobs will still be needed for a long time to come.

We have argued that the international environment within which the present growth in structural unemployment has occurred is fundamentally different from the one even ten years ago, which we discussed in Freeman *et al.* (1982) or Freeman and Soete (1987). As increasingly recognised in many policy circles, the world of the 1990s is a much different world from the 1980s. The entry of an important group of newcomers from South East Asia has significantly altered international competitive relations. This international competitive trend is, however, only the first indication of a much more fundamental trend involving a shift in growth pole from the North Atlantic to the South East Asian and Pacific Rim area. It is a trend which will benefit the world as a whole, bringing about many new market growth and export opportunities to Northern countries. These opportunities will require, however, more skills, more knowledge from those firms located in the North. The growth of South and East Asia with their huge reservoir of unskilled labour will tend to make unskilled labour in the rich Northern economies uncompetitive in the traded economy at basically whatever minimum wage.

The enormous potential offered by ICT for international communication and relocation is likely, as we argued in Chapter 4, to increase the international tradability of many routine jobs in service sectors which were hitherto untradable or 'sheltered'. In so far as the international transport of such immaterial goods and activities is nearly costless and has very limited environmental costs, it is likely to accelerate the accompanying process of international 'unskilled labour wage equalisation'.

On a still more speculative note, the 'shrinking' of the, until now, untradable or sheltered economy sector is not likely to be limited to simple routine jobs. The heavy investments in education over the last 20–30 years in many South and East Asian economies will pay off even more. The available human capital in these countries is in some instances higher than in the OECD countries. As we argued in Chapter 4, a case could be made therefore that there will be a widening of the international 'wage equalisation' process to many more occupations and low to medium skills (such as basic programming skills, etc.) Again, the question can be raised whether this process of international competition from the South has led or is likely to lead to a similar process of competing away of a number of basic skills, and becoming a major factor behind the rapid growth in unemployment of such basic occupations and skills in Northern economies, such as Europe. It is for this reason that we have put great stress both on high-skill competitive sectors in Europe *and* on a new sheltered non-tradable sector.

Another fundamental change in the world economy has been the collapse of the centrally planned economies in Eastern Europe. In many respects, this development simply intensifies the problems raised with respect to Eastern Asia. However, whereas the Asian countries are highly competitive and growing fast, the East European countries face the danger of an even greater unemployment crisis than that experienced by Western Europe, with all the tragic consequences which could follow in terms of ethnic conflicts, crime, social and political turmoil, militaristic nationalist regimes.

There is therefore an urgent need for the international community to assist the Eastern European countries also to handle their transition to ICT-based economies in such a way as to avoid long-term mass unemployment. This would require not simply market reforms of the type which have constantly been urged but also a supply-side programme for structural change and infrastructural investment, resembling in many ways the post-war Marshall Plan for Western Europe in its scale and scope. The 50th Anniversary of General Marshall's historic speech could well be the occasion for launching such a plan. It would be very much in the interests of the OECD countries from the standpoint of their own economic growth and employment, as well as that of Eastern Europe and the world economy as a whole.

From this brief and necessarily simplified discussion it is evident that the *international* dimensions of handling the unemployment problems of Western Europe are even more daunting than the domestic problems. Nevertheless, as Keynes, more than any other twentieth century economist, showed, the two aspects are inseparably linked. Although he was the chief architect of the Bretton Woods system which ushered in a quarter of a century of stable growth and full employment in many countries, he nevertheless was disappointed that the international economic institutions which he helped to design were not even more ambitious. A return to his concepts on an international scale will be needed more than ever in the coming century, including the forgotten points of his agenda, such as more ambitious support for Third World development. A vertebrate world economy à la Bretton Woods will be needed to provide a stable framework for trade, investment and growth. But as in domestic affairs, the role of technology in structural change cannot be ignored.

International economic institutions will need to concern themselves increasingly with technology transfer and world-wide infrastructures in telecommunications, as well as education, technological infrastructure and R&D.

In this short book we cannot address in depth all the problems of the international economy. We have attempted to show the relevance of the diffusion of ICT to the world-wide process of structural change in which we are all engulfed. Not surprisingly, the policy concerns have shifted in the 1990s from a belief in the largely automatic macro-economic and labour market employment compensation mechanisms to a much more active neo-Keynesian agenda both in international affairs and in domestic policies for employment creation, new infrastructural investments and demand management. The Clinton–Gore plans and the Delors White Paper bring to the forefront, sometimes implicitly, sometimes explicitly, the need for such policy proposals to be framed in the much broader neo-Schumpeterian growth framework, which we have attempted to outline in this book and which is as relevant on a global as on a national scale.

REFERENCES

Arrow, K. J. (1994), 'Problems mount in application of free market economic theory', *Guardian,* 4 January.

Arthur, W. B. (1988), 'Competing technologies: an overview', in G. Dosi *et al.* (eds), *Technical Change and Economic Theory*, London, Pinter.

Baba, Y., Takai, S. and Mizuta, Y. (1994), 'The evolution of the software industry in Japan: a comprehensive analysis', in D. Mowery (ed.), *The International Computer Software Industry*, Oxford, Oxford University Press.

Babbage, C. (1832), *On the Economy of Machinery and Manufactures*, 4th Edition (1835), reprinted by Frank Cass, London (1963).

Balassa, B. (1961), *The Theory of Economic Integration*, Homewood, Illinois.

Beale, N. and Nethercott, S. (1986), 'Job loss and health: the influence of age and previous morbidity', *Journal of Royal College of General Practitioners,* vol. 36, pp. 261–4.

Bell, D. (1974), *The Coming of Post-Industrial Society*, London, Heinemann.

Bengtsson, J. (1993), Labour markets of the future: the challenge to education policy makers, *European Journal of Education,* vol. 28, no. 2, pp. 135–57.

Berg, M. (1987), 'Babbage', in J. Eatwell *et al.* (eds), *The New Palgrave Dictionary of Economics,* vol. 1, London, Macmillan.

Beveridge, W. H. (1931), *Causes and Cures of Unemployment,* London, Longmans Green.

Beveridge, W. H. (1942), *Social Insurance and Allied Services,* Cmnd 6404, HMSO.

Beveridge, W. H. (1944), *Full Employment in a Free Society,* London, Allen and Unwin.

Blanchard, O. and Diamond, P. (1988), *Unemployment and Wages: What Have We Learned from the European Experience?* London, The Employment Institute.

Boyer, R. (1988), 'Technical change and the Theory of Regulation', in G. Dosi *et al.* (eds), *Technical Change and Economic Theory,* London, Pinter.

Boyer, R. (1989), Synthesis Report: New Directions in Management, OECD Helsinki Conference on Education Practices and Work Organisation: Technological Change as a Social Process, 11–13 December, Paris, OECD.

Boyer, R. (1993), 'Ressources humaines, nouveaux modèles productifs et emploi', paper presented at OECD Helsinki Conference on Technology, Innovation Policy and Employment, 7–9 October, Paris, OECD.

Boyer, R. and Caroli, E. (1993), 'Production regimes, education and training systems', paper presented to RAND Conference on Human Capital, 17 November, Santa Barbara, RAND.

Brenner, M. H. (1987), 'Economic change, alcohol consumption and heart disease mortality in nine industrialised countries', *Social Science and Medicine,* vol. 25, pp. 119–32.

Brooks, H. (1973), *Science, Growth and Society* (Brooks Report), Paris, OECD.

Browning, H. C. and Singelman, J. (1978), 'The transformation of the US labour force', *Politics and Society,* vol. 8, pp. 481–509.

Brynjolfsson, E. (1991), *Information Technology and the Productivity Paradox: What We Know and What We Don't Know*, Cambridge, MIT Sloan School.

Burchell, B. (1992), 'Towards a social psychology of the labour market or why we need to understand the labour market before we can understand unemployment', *Journal of Occupational and Organisational Psychology*, vol. 65, pp. 345–54.

Business Week (1993), 14 June.

Cassiolato, J. (1992), 'The user-producer connection in hi-tech: a case study of banking automation in Brazil', in H. Schmitz and J. Cassiolato (eds), *High Tech for Industrial Development*, London, Routledge.

Cawson, A., Haddon, L. and Miles, I. (1994, forthcoming), *The Shape of Things to Consume: Bringing Information Technology into the Home*, London, Pinter.

CEC (1993), *Growth, Competitiveness, Employment*, White Paper (Delors Report), December, Brussels, CEC.

Clinton, W. J. and Gore, A. (1993), *Technology for America's Economic Growth: A New Direction to Build Economic Strength*, President's Office, Washington.

Cole, G. D. H. (1948), *A Short History of the British Working Class Movement*, London, Allen and Unwin.

Cooper, C. M. and Clark, J. A. (1982), *Employment, Economics and Technology: The Impact of Technical Change on the Labour Market*, Brighton, Wheatsheaf.

Datamation (1990, 1991, 1992, 1993), 'The Datamation 100'.

David, P. (1982), 'Comments', in ICCP, *Micro-electronics, Robots and Jobs*, no. 7, Paris, OECD, p. 148.

David, P. and Bunn, J. A. (1988), 'The economics of gateway technologies: network evolution and the lessons from the electricity supply industry, *Information Economics and Policy*, vol. 5, pp. 165–202.

David, P. and Steinmüller, E. (1990), 'The ISDN bandwagon is coming but who will be there to climb aboard?', *Economics of Innovation and New Technology*, vol. 1, no. 1, pp. 43–62.

Devine, W. (1983), 'From shafts to wires', *Journal of Economic History*, vol. 43, no. 2, pp. 347–73.

de Witt, G. R. (1990), 'A review of the literature on technological change and employment', European Commission, DGs V and XIII, Brussels.

Dickinson, D. (1994), 'Crime and unemployment', Department of Applied Economics, Cambridge University.

Diebold, J. (1952), *Automation: The Advent of the Automatic Factory*, New York, Van Norstrand.

Dobb, M. (1946), *Studies in the Development of Capitalism*, London, Routledge.

Dosi, G. (1982), 'Technological paradigms and technological trajectories', *Research Policy*, vol. 11, no. 3, pp. 147–62.

Dosi, G., Freeman, C., Nelson, R., Silverberg, G., and Soete, L. (eds) (1988) *Technical Change and Economic Theory*, London, Pinter.

Eatwell, J. (1982), *Whatever Happened to Britain?*, London, Duckworth/BBC.

Economist (1993), Editorial, 17 July.

Eliasson, G. (1992), 'Business competence, organisational learning and economic growth', in F. Scherer and M. Perlman (eds), *Entrepreneurship, Innovation and Economic Growth*, Ann Arbor, University of Michigan Press, pp. 251–77.

Etzioni, A. (1993), *The Parenting Deficit*, London, DEMOS.

Financial Times (1993), 4 August.

Financial Times (1993), 4 November.

Financial Times (1994), 16 February.

Finch, J. (1994), 'The price we are paying for the rise of new technology', *Daily Express*, 1 February.

Fineman, S. (1987), 'Back to employment: wounds and wisdoms', in D. Fryer and P. Ullah (eds), *Unemployed People*, Milton Keynes, Open University Press, pp. 268–84.

Fleck, J. (1988), *Innofusion or Diffusation: The Nature of Technological Development in Robotics*, University of Edinburgh, PICT Working Paper No. 4.

Fleck, J. (1993), 'Configurations crystallising contingency', *The International Journal of Human Factors in Manufacturing*, vol. 3, no. 1, pp. 15–36.

Foray, D. and Freeman, C. (eds) (1993), *Technology and the Wealth of Nations*, London, Pinter.

Fox, R. and Guagnini, A. (1993), *Education, Technology and Industrial Performance, 1856–1939*, Cambridge, Cambridge University Press.

Freeman, C. (1982), *The Economics of Industrial Innovation*, London, Pinter.

Freeman, C. (1984), 'Prometheus Unbound', *Futures*, October, pp. 494–507.

Freeman, C. (1992), *The Economics of Hope*, London, Pinter.

Freeman, C. (ed.) (1994 forthcoming), *Long Waves in The World Economy*, International Library of Critical Writings in Economics, Aldershot, Elgar.

Freeman, C., Clark, J. and Soete, L. (1982), *Unemployment and Technical Innovation: A Study of Long Waves and Economic Development*, London, Pinter.

Freeman, C. and Perez, C. (1988), 'Structural crises of adjustment, business cycles and investment behaviour', in G. Dosi *et al.* (eds), *Technical Change and Economic Theory*, London, Pinter.

Freeman, C. and Soete, L. (1987), *Technical Change and Full Employment*, Oxford, Blackwell.

Fryer, D. M. and Payne, R. L. (1986), 'Being unemployed: review of the literature on the psychological experience of unemployment', in G. L. Cooper and I. Robertson (eds), *International Review of Industrial and Organisational Psychology*, pp. 235–78.

Galbraith, J. K. (1954), *The Great Crash 1929*, London, Hamilton (Penguin Edition, Harmondsworth, 1955).

Galbraith, J. K. (1992), *The Culture of Contentment*, London, Sinclair Stevenson.

Gann, D. (1992), *Intelligent Buildings, Producers and Users*, University of Sussex, SPRU.

GATT (1990), *International Trade*, Volume II, Geneva.

Gershuny, J. (1994 forthcoming), *Changing Times*, Oxford, Oxford University Press.

Gilder, G. (1993), 'The death of telephony' in 'The Future Surveyed', *Economist*, London, 11 September, pp. 91–5.

Gourvitch, A. (1940), *Survey of Economic Theory on Technological Change and Employment*, New York, A. M. Kelley.

Grübler, A. (1990), *The Rise and Fall of Infrastructures: Dynamics of Evolution and Technological Change in Transport*, Heidelberg, Physica Verlag.

Guy, K. (1987), 'The UK tertiary service sector' in C. Freeman and L. Soete (eds), *Technical Change and Full Employment*, Oxford, Blackwell.

Haddon, L. and Silverstone, R. (1994), *Teleworking in the 1990s: a view from the home*, SPRU CICT Research Report Series no. 10, CICT, University of Sussex.

Hanly, C. (1989), *The Age of Unreason*, London, Century Hutchinson.

Havas, A. (1993), The Hungarian Laser Industry in Transition, 19th Congress of EARIE, Stuttgart.

Hayek, F. (1980), *1980s, Unemployment and the Unions*, Hobart Paper No. 87, London, Institute of Economic Affairs.

Heckscher, E. (1935), *Mercantilism*, London, Allen and Unwin.

Henkoff, R. (1991), 'Making your office more productive', *Fortune*, 25 February, pp. 74–80.

Hewitt, P. (1993), *About Time: The Revolution in Work and Family Life*, London, IPPR/Rivers Oram Press.

Holland, S. (1993), *The European Imperative: Economic and Social Cohesion in the 1990s: A Report to the CEC*, Nottingham, Spokesman.

Hutchinson, T. W. (1977), *Keynes vs. the Keynesians*, London, Institute of Economic Affairs.

International Herald Tribune (1993), 27 July.

ILO (1989), *Conditions of Work Digest: Part-Time Work,* Geneva, International Labour Office.

ILO (1992), *Yearbook of Labour Statistics,* Geneva, International Labour Office.

Jackson, T. (1994), 'Either get smarter or else get poorer', *Financial Times,* 25 February.

Jahoda, M. (1982), *Employment and Unemployment: A Social Psychological Analysis,* Cambridge, Cambridge University Press.

Jahoda, M. (1987), 'Unemployment: facts, experience and social consequences', in C. Freeman and L. Soete (eds), *Technical Change and Full Employment,* Oxford, Blackwell.

Jahoda, M. (1993) 'Social psychological consequences of unemployment', internal memo, University of Sussex, SPRU.

Jahoda, M., Lazarsfeld, P. F. and Zeisel, H. (1933), *Marienthal: The Sociography of an Unemployed Community* (English translation 1972), London, Tavistock Publications.

Jensen, L. M. and Kjeldsen-Kragh, M. (1994), 'Job creation in the consumer services sector', Copenhagen, Ministry of Industry and Business Coordination.

Johnson, B. and Lundvall, B.-A. (1992), Chapter 2 in B.-A. Lundvall (ed.), *National Systems of Innovation,* London, Pinter, pp. 18–36.

Juliussen, K. P. and Juliussen, E. (1993), *The 6th Annual Computer Industry Almanac,* Austin, Texas, Reference Press Inc.

Kalecki, M. (1943), 'Political aspects of full employment', *Political Quarterly,* October.

Katz, B. G. and Phillips, A. (1982), 'Government, technological opportunities and the emergence of the computer industry', in H. Giersch, (ed.), *Emerging Technologies,* Tübingen, J. C. B. Mohr.

Kemp, R. and Soete, L. (1992), 'The greening of technological progress: an evolutionary perspective', *Futures,* vol. 24, no. 5, pp. 437–57.

Kettle, J. (1993), 'Working in Canada', *Newsletter*, Society for the Reduction of Human Labor, vol. 3, no. 3, pp. 5–8.

Keynes, J. M. (1923), *Tract on Monetary Reform*, as reprinted in *Collected Writings* (1971), Vol. IV, London, Macmillan and Royal Economic Society.

Keynes, J. M. (1930), *Treatise on Money*, London, Macmillan.

Keynes, J. M. (1931), 'The end of laissez-faire', in *Essays in Persuasion*, London, Macmillan.

Keynes, J. M. (1936), *General Theory of Employment, Interest and Money*, New York, Harcourt Brace.

Kirby, T. (1994), 'Jobless link to crime suppressed', *The Independent*, 8 April.

Kondratieff, N. (1925), 'The long wave in economic life', English translation in *Review of Economic Statistics*, vol. 17, pp. 105–15.

Layard, R. and Nickell, S. (1985) 'The causes of British unemployment', *National Institute Economic Review*, February, pp. 62–85.

Layard, R. and Philpot, J. (1991), *Stopping Unemployment*, London, The Employment Institute.

Lichtenberg. F. R. (1993), *The output contribution of computer equipment and personnel: a firm-level analysis*, Working Paper No. 4540, Cambridge Mass., National Bureau of Economic Research.

Lippman, J. (1993), 'They've seen the future and switched channels', *New York Herald Tribune*, 1 September.

Lovio, R. (1994), *Evolution of Firm Communities in New Industries: The Case of the Finnish Electronics Industry*, Helsinki, Helsinki School of Economics.

Lucas, R. F. B. (1988), 'On the mechanisms of economic development', *Journal of Monetary Economics*, vol. 22, pp. 3–42.

Lundvall, B.-A. and Petit, P. (1993), 'Technology and employment: contemporary issues', CEPREMAP, mimeo.

McCracken Report (1977), *Towards Full Employment and Price Stability*, Paris, OECD.

Machlup, F. (1962), *The Production and Distribution of Knowledge in the United States*, Princeton, Princeton University Press.

Macrae, N. (1994) 'The Jolly Roger flies for full employment', *Sunday Times*, 20 March.

Maddison, A. (1980), 'Western economic performance in the 1970s', *Banco Nazionale del Lavoro, Quarterly Review*, no. 134, pp. 247–89.

Maddison, A. (1982), *Phases of Capitalist Development*, Oxford, Oxford University Press.

Maddison, A. (1991), *Dynamic Forces in Capitalist Development: A Long Run Comparative View*, Oxford, Oxford University Press.

Mansell, R. (1993), *The New Telecommunications: A Political Economy of Network Evolution*, London, Sage.

Mansell, R. and Jenkins, M. (1992), 'Networks, industrial and restructuring policy: the Singapore example', *Technovation*, vol. 12, no. 6, pp. 397–406.

Marshall, A. (1890), *Principles of Economics*, 8th Edition (1920), London, Macmillan, p. 536.

Marx, K. (1848), *The Communist Manifesto*, recent edition in D. McLellan (ed.), *Karl Marx Selected Writings*, Oxford, Oxford University Press.

Mensch, G. (1975), *Das technologische Patt: Innovationen überwinden Depression*, Frankfurt, Umschau.

Meyer-Krahmer, F. (1992), 'The effects of new technologies on employment', *Economics of Innovation and New Technology*, vol. 2, pp. 131–49.

Moggridge, D. E. (1976), *Keynes*, London, Fontana.

Montrol, E. E. and Badger, W. W. (1974), *Introduction to Quantatitive Aspects of Social Phenomena*, New York, Gordon and Breach.

Nakicenovic, N. (1986), 'The automobile road to technological change: diffusion of the automobile as a process of technological substitution', *Technological Forecasting and Social Change*, vol. 29, pp. 309–40.

Nakicenovic, N. (1988), 'Dynamics and replacement of US transport infrastructures', in J. H. Ausubel and R. Herman (eds), *Cities and Their Vital Systems: Infrastructure, Past, Present and Future*, Washington, DC, National Academy Press.

Nelson, R. R. (ed.) (1993), *National Innovations Systems: a Comparative Analysis*, New York, Oxford University Press.

Nelson, R. and Winter, S. (1982), *An Evolutionary Theory of Economic Change*, Cambridge, MA, Harvard University Press.

Nye, D. E. (1990), *Electrifying America*, Cambridge, Mass., MIT Press.

Oakley, B. (1990), 'Trends in the European IT skills scene', Pergamon Infotech, London, Conference on Human Resource Development in IT, 19–21 February.

OECD (1990, 1992 and 1993), *Employment Outlook*, Paris, OECD.

OECD (1992), *Education at a Glance*, Paris, OECD.

OECD (1993), *The OECD Response*, Interim Report by the Secretary General on Employment/Unemployment, OECD, June 1993, Paris.

Olson, M. (1982), *The Rise and Decline of Nations*, New Haven, Yale University Press.

Ormerod, P. (1994), *The Death of Economics*, London, Faber and Faber.

Panko, R. R. (1991), 'Is office productivity stagnant?' *MIS Quarterly*, June, pp. 191–203.

Pasinetti, L. (1981), *Structural Change and Economic Growth*, Cambridge, Cambridge University Press.

Pavitt, K. (1986), 'Chips and trajectories: how does the semi-conductor influence the direction of technical change?' in R. Macleod (ed.), *Technology and the Human Prospect*, London, Pinter.

Perez, C. (1983), 'Structural change and the assimilation of new technologies in the economic and social system', *Futures*, vol. 15, no. 5, pp. 357–75.

Perez, C. (1985), 'Micro-electronics, long waves and world structural change: new perspectives for developing countries', *World Development*, vol. 13, no. 3, pp. 441–63.

Perez, C. (1990), *Technical change, competitive restructuring and institutional reform*, World Bank Strategic Planning Paper No. 4, Washington, DC, World Bank.

Petit, P. (1993), 'Technology and employment: the main issues', OECD Conference on Technology, Innovation Policy and Employment, Helsinki, 7–9 October, Paris, OECD.

Petty, W. (1690), *Verbum Sapienti*, republished in C. H. Hull, (ed.) *Economic Writings* (1899), Cambridge, Cambridge University Press.

Phelps-Brown, H. (1975), 'A non-monetarist view of the pay explosion', *Three Banks Review*, no. 105.

Poon, A. (1993), *Tourism, Technology and Competitive Strategies*, Wallingford, CAB International.

Prais, S. J. (1987), 'Educating for productivity: comparisons of Japanese and English schooling and vocational preparation', *National Institute Economic Review*, no. 119, February.

Prais, S. J. (1989), 'Qualified manpower in engineering: Britain and other industrially advanced countries', *National Institute Economic Review*, no. 127, February.

Quinn, J. (1986), 'The impacts of technology in the service sector', Symposium on World Technology, NAE, Washington, DC, 13–16 February.

Quintas, P. (1994), 'Paths of innovation in software and system development practice', in R. Mansell (ed.), *Emerging Patterns of Control: The Management of Information and Communications Technologies*, London, Aslib.

Rasch, R. H. and Tosi, H. L. (1992), 'Factors affecting software development performance: an integrated approach', *MIS Quarterly*, vol 16, no. 3, pp. 395–413.

Ricardo, D. (1821), *Principles of Political Economy and Taxation* (Third Edition) in P. Sraffa (ed.), *The Works and Correspondence of David Ricardo*, Vol. 1, Cambridge, Cambridge University Press.

Romer, P. M. (1986), 'Increasing returns and long-run growth', *Journal of Political Economy*, vol. 94, pp. 1002–37.

Romer, P. M. (1990), 'Endogenous technological change', *Journal of Political Economy*, vol. 98, S71–S102.

Rosenberg, N. (1976), *Perspectives in Technology*, Cambridge, Cambridge University Press.

Rosted, J. (1993), 'The employment objective: what is the appropriate link between macro-economic policies and innovation policy?' Conference on Technology, Innovation Policy and Employment, Helsinki, 7–9 October, Paris, OECD.

Rothwell, R., Freeman, C., Horlsey, A., Jervis, V. T. P., Robertson, A. B. and Townsend, J. (1974), SAPPHO Updated: Project SAPPHO Phase II, *Research Policy*, vol. 3, no. 3, pp. 258–91.

Sakurai, N. (1993), 'Structural change and employment: empirical evidence for eight OECD countries', paper prepared for Helsinki Conference on Technology, Innovation Policy and Employment, 7–9 October, Paris, OECD.

Salvati, M. (1984), 'Political business cycles and long waves in industrial relations: notes on Kalecki and Phelps-Brown', in C. Freeman (ed.) *Long Waves in the World Economy*, London, Pinter.

Samuelson, P. (1980), *Economics*, 11th Edition, New York, McGraw-Hill.

Samuelson, P. A. (1981), 'The World's economy at century's end', *Japan Economic Journal*, 10 March, p. 20.

Schumpeter, J. (1939), *Business Cycles: A Theoretical, Historical and Statistical Analysis*, New York, McGraw Hill.

Schumpeter, J. (1943), *Capitalism, Socialism and Democracy*, 6th Edition, 1987, London, Unwin Paperbacks.

Schumpeter, J. (1952), *Ten Great Economists*, London, Allen and Unwin.

Sherman, B. and Jenkins, C. (1979), *The Collapse of Work*, London, Eyre Methuen.

Sherman, B. and Judkins, P. (1992), *Glimpses of Heaven, Visions of Hell: Virtual Reality and its Implications*, London, Hodder and Stoughton.

Simonetti, R. (1993), 'The long-run performance of large firms: a study of changes in the "Fortune" list 1964–1988', University of Sussex, SPRU, mimeo.

Smith, A. (1776), *Inquiry into the Nature and Causes of the Wealth of Nations*, Everyman Edition (1910), London, J. M. Dent.

Solomou, S. (1987), *Phases of Economic Growth, 1850–1973*, Cambridge, Cambridge University Press.

Statistical Abstract (1992), Washington, DC, United States Government Printing Office.

Steuart, J. (1767), *An Inquiry into the Principles of Political Economy*, London, Millar and Cadell.

Sunday Telegraph (1994), 'Tories end love affair with motor car', 13 March.

Swanson, K. *et al.* (1991), 'The application software factory: applying total quality techniques to systems development', *MIS Quarterly*, vol. 5, no. 4, pp. 567–78.

The Times (1994), 21 February.

UNCTAD *Handbook of Trade and Development Statistics* (1976, 1983, 1982–90), Geneva and New York.

United States Bureau of Labor Statistics (1991), Bulletin 2370, Washington, DC, US Government Printing Office.

United States Bureau of Labor Statistics (1992), *Outlook 1990–2005. Projections of US Labour Force Occupations*, Bulletin 2402, Washington, DC, US Government Printing Office.

van der Zwan, A. (1979), 'On the assessment of the Kondratieff cycle', Centre for Business Research, Erasmus University, Rotterdam.

van Gelderen, J. (1913), 'Springvloed Beschouwingen over industriële Ontwikkeling en prijsbeweging', *De Nieuwe Tijd*, vol. 184, nos. 5 and 6, English translation.

Verspagen, B. (1994), 'Kondratieff cycles' (translation), in C. Freeman (ed.), *Long Waves in the World Economy*, (forthcoming), Aldershot, Elgar.

Vivarelli, M. (1994, forthcoming), *Technology and Employment: The Economic Theory and the Empirical Evidence*, London.

von Mises, L. (1936), *Socialism*, London, Jonathan Cape, p. 485.

von Tunzelmann, N. (1993), 'Time-Saving Technical Change: the cotton industry in the English industrial revolution', University of Sussex, SPRU, mimeo.

Warr, P. (1983), 'Work, jobs and unemployment', *Bulletin of the British Psychological Society*, vol. 36, pp. 305–34.

Wheelan, C. T. (1992), 'The role of income, life-style deprivation and financial strain in mediating the impact of unemployment on psychological distress: evidence from the Republic of Ireland', *Journal of Occupational and Organisational Psychology*, vol. 65, pp. 331–44.

Wiener, N. (1949), *The Human Use of Human Beings: A Cybernetic Approach*, New York, Houghton Mifflin.

Wiggenhorn, W. (1990), 'Motorola University: when training becomes education', *Harvard Business Review*, vol. 68, no. 4, July–August.

Williams, B. (1984), *Shorter Hours, Increased Employment* (Three Banks Review, September), reprint of OECD, Conference Paper, Paris.

Wood, A. (1994), *North–South Trade Employment and Inequality: Changing Fortunes in a Skill-Driven World*, Oxford, Clarendon Press.

World Bank (1993), *East Asian Miracle*, Washington, DC, World Bank.

Worswick, G. D. N. (1991), *Unemployment: A Problem of Policy*, Cambridge, Cambridge University Press.

INDEX